WRITING
YOUR OWN
PLAYS

WRITING YOUR OWN PLAYS

○○○○○○○○○○○○○○○○○○○○○○○○

Creating · Adapting
Improvising

○○○○○○○○○○○○○○○○○○○○○○○○

CAROL KORTY

CHARLES SCRIBNER'S SONS · NEW YORK

Charles Scribner's Sons Books for Young Readers
Macmillan Publishing Company
866 Third Avenue, New York, NY 10022
Collier Macmillan Canada, Inc.

Printed in the United States of America
First Edition
10 9 8 7 6 5 4 3 2 1

Library of Congress Cataloging-in-Publication Data
Korty, Carol.   Writing your own plays.
Bibliography: p.   Includes index.
Summary: Identifies the characteristics of a play and gives guidelines, suggestions, and examples for choosing a story, developing ideas, making a first draft, adapting to practical considerations, and preparing the finished script.
1. Playwriting—Juvenile literature. [1. Playwriting.
2. Creative writing] I. Title.
PN1661.K58   1986   808.2   86-21969
ISBN 0-684-18470-2

To my mother, my grandmother, and my aunt,
who read me stories by the hour when I was young.

Thanks and Acknowledgments to

Emerson College, which has supported me in my work.

The Maurice J. Tobin School in Boston, where students, teachers, administrators were open to the process.

Institute for the Arts, in Boston, which funded me as a playwright-in-residence.

Virginia Center for the Creative Arts, where I drafted this book.

Anita and Alex Page, who gave me feedback on the manuscript.

Wilford Leach, who got me to write plays.

John Braswell, who gave me moral support when I began.

Remy Charlip, who helped me find my sources for ideas.

Antioch College, which taught me to question and to think and developed me as a teacher and an artist.

Sarah Lawrence College, which developed me as an artist.

State University College of New York at Brockport, which supported my creativity.

Peace lovers everywhere, who support the spirit of life.

Lovers of life, who support the Spirit.

CONTENTS

FOREWORD
Why Write a Play?

You must have heard people say, "Oh, that would make a good play!" Perhaps they say it about a situation they're witnessing, or an adventure they've just heard a friend describe, or a newspaper article they've read. What is this urge to turn an incident or a story into a play? Making the events of our lives into a story seems to be a way of remembering what has happened to us and of sharing our thoughts and feelings about life with others. But why a play?

I believe the urge to make a play comes from the desire to go beyond enjoying an experience in our own minds to sharing it in communion with others. Sharing an event in communion means experiencing it in common with others at the same time. Everyone is focusing on the same thing at once, even though individual reactions might be different. When a play **works** * well, the event becomes more important than when it was private, and you feel a bond between the people watching and the people playing. This is what makes theater. It's fun when the play is funny. It's comfort-

---

* Words printed in bold type are defined in the Glossary beginning on page 96.

ing when events are sad. There is something quite wonderful about performing and watching a play together. Not only are you sharing an event in your life, you're sharing ideas and feelings about what it is to live life.

Having the urge to share a story or an experience is not quite the same thing, however, as actually taking on the project of making a play from it. This means getting down to some real work that can be as difficult as it is exciting. Do you want to put on a play but have no script or ideas yet? Is there a story you love and want to share with others in play form? Do you have a script that needs some changes to make it more interesting or to make it fit your group of actors? Do you just enjoy writing and want to try your hand at a play?

Whatever your objective, this book is intended to help you with suggestions, examples, questions, and points to consider. If anything here gets you going or puts you back on track when you're stuck, by all means use it! If something doesn't make sense to you or doesn't work for you, don't worry; keep looking for something that does. Creative work is impossible to understand fully. You aren't the only one with questions and doubts! We can give one another guidelines and "rules" to help, but no one will accept or agree with all of them. In **playwriting** there are no exact answers as there are in mathematics. The suggestions in this book come from my own experience reading, directing, and making plays. I've written them down as much to help myself understand the process as to help you! We never finish learning how to write a good play.

1

A Play Is Different from a Story

You can tell as soon as you look at a written page whether you have a play or a story before you. A story is written in narrative form, has descriptions, and its dialogue is in quotation marks. A story can be told in the past tense, in the present, or even in the future. But the script for a play always makes the events happen in the present, and it tells you primarily what the **characters** are saying, plus some brief notes about what people are doing and where the action takes place. When you see a play being acted out or hear a story being told, you have no trouble telling which is which. Seeing people act out what characters are doing is very different from having a person tell you about what happened to someone.

There is a very important similarity between stories and plays, however: they both tell a tale about life. When we think back on a tale we have seen or read or heard, we don't always recall the **form** through which we received it but just remember the particular character and what happened to him or her. This is fine; it means the form was

1

"working," that is, it was effective in getting us to focus on what happened.

There is a value, however, in having different forms through which to tell a tale. Some ideas are better captured in story form and some in play form. For this reason it is useful to spend a little time thinking about the difference between the two. It will make it easier for you, the artist, to pick your material and to make choices as you develop your play.

Plays are meant, of course, to be performed, and stories to be read or told. A play *shows* the audience what the characters do. A story *tells* the reader or listener about the characters and what they do, and the action happens in the listener's imagination. Because action is the most basic ingredient of plays, a **playwright** always needs to focus on how people do things. **Action** is the means for telling a tale in play form. Stories, on the other hand, don't always have to deal with action; they can be about things people think or feel or experience inside. This is called the inner life of a character. Good plays also tell us of the inner life of a character, but they have to find ways to show us this through the character's action.

Action in a play is not really the same as activity. Action is what characters do in order to accomplish their main desire or **objective** in the play. It might be physically active or it might not. For example, in the play *Macbeth* by William Shakespeare, the main character, Macbeth, wants to become king. In some scenes of the play, Macbeth is very physically active in going after his objective, such as when he fights Macduff, who opposes his plan. In other scenes, however, he uses quiet treachery, such as warmly welcom-

2

ing the king, Duncan, into his castle in order to create an opportunity for murdering him.

A character will often have different objectives during different scenes in the play; these relate to his or her overall desire or objective. What the character does to get what he or she wants makes up the action of the play. Watching this action unfold is what makes the play interesting—funny, suspenseful, sad, exciting. Action is the means of telling a tale in play form. A play does not just tell you about the way things are or what a character would like to do, as a story might. A play shows us people doing things to get what they want.

Another difference between plays and stories is the way time is used. A story does not have restrictions on the amount of time it covers. It might deal with five minutes of thoughts and feelings in a person's head or it might deal with events that occur over many, many years. It can jump from past to present in any fashion. A play tends to work best when its time frame is restricted to a fairly short period. Some playwrights have found ways to make effective leaps in time by using flashbacks or by jumping ahead ten or twenty years, showing us how a person's life moves along. It is hard to do this successfully, however, without lessening the dramatic tension between characters as they jump the years.

A long series of events can be interesting when recounted in a story but boring in a play because no situation would be lengthy enough to let the playwright develop interesting relationships between characters or actions for them to play. A story can make you visualize complicated action by just a few words and phrases that spark your

3

imagination, but a play must *show* you what a character does. Showing action takes much longer than telling, so you can't move the **plot** ahead in a play as fast as you can in a story. If you try to hurry it and your play fails to develop interaction between characters, you will have missed the real stuff that good plays are made of.

Not only the *time* but the *places* in which events occur must be restricted in plays. Stories can tell you about many different places and can easily move the scene from indoors to outdoors, from one country to another, from sea to woods to mountains, in a few sentences. Think how hard it is to do that in a play! Films, television, and radio plays can make these switches, but plays for the stage must limit their use of **location.**

Many playwrights solve the problem by using methods that do not call for realistic scenery. Blocks, screens, and shapes are used by actors to represent a city street, a space-ship, a recording studio, or a prairie. This theatrical approach opens many possibilities. Even if you free yourself from the complication and expense of changing spaces and times, however, it is still better for artistic reasons to limit yourself to a few **locales** in order to develop the characters and the action well. Good dramas give you more in the depth and complexity of dramatic action between characters than in the quantity of events, places, and people.

A final point about the difference between plays and stories concerns their finished form. The written story is considered the finished piece. The finished version of a play is not the **script,** however; it is the performance of the script. This is true of all performing arts. The movements of a dance score, the notes of a music score, the words of a play

4

are the creation of the choreographer, the composer, or the playwright and are meant to be brought to life by the dancer, musician, or actor. In literary arts such as stories, novels, and poems, the artist speaks directly to his or her audience through the work of art he or she creates. This is also true of visual arts such as sculpture and painting. But performing arts involve the important middle step of interpretation by performing artists. In theater, this could be as simple as actors becoming the characters of the script, playing the action, and creating the environment as they act. It could also be a very complicated production involving not only actors but also a scene designer, a costume designer, a lighting designer, a sound designer, a make-up designer, a composer, all contributing to the interpretation of the playwright's script. So as you create your script, keep in mind the fact that other artists will be bringing the **piece** to life in performance. The writing process for a play, therefore, is quite different from writing a story for someone to read.

The script of the play is a recipe for action. It is not the finished product any more than a recipe for a good soup is the real soup. Someone who knows something about theater or cooking can read a recipe or a script and imagine what the finished product would be like. Their imaginations enable them to say, "This is great!" or "I don't like this; it's not worth working on." They are responding as audience, already experiencing the characters in action or tasting the soup. Every step of the way in theater involves imagination. The playwright imagines a play and writes a script that will stimulate performing artists to imagine how they'll bring it to life; the combined work of the artists then stimulates the imagination of the audience as they experience the performance of the play.

Fortunately, you don't have to worry about how the script will work on everyone's imagination when you are writing. It is enough just to let that ride in the back of your mind as you come up with a situation, characters, and action that capture what you want to say. If it feels right to you, the original creator, it will probably work for any of the other people who want to use the script. Do keep in mind, however, that what you say needs to be put in terms of action. The play you write will tell its tale through characters doing things; these characters will be brought to life by **actors** performing for an audience.

∘∘∘ 2 ∘∘∘

Choosing a Story

When you're first beginning to write plays, it often helps you get started to think in terms of turning a story into a play. That's because we tend to think of events that happen to people in terms of a story. The story, of course, could be from a book or from real life or just an idea you have. Once you're clear about how to adapt a play from a story, it may be easier for you to create a play from scratch without first thinking of story form. Chapter Ten discusses this.

The story you choose to work on needs to be one you really like. Something about it should excite you. It might be the characters, or even just one character, that appeal to you. The situation of the story might make you laugh, or move you, or make you angry. Maybe it gave you an image that has stuck in your mind—something that you vividly can see happening in front of your eyes. Perhaps the message of the whole tale is one you feel says something important about life—your life or all human life. Whatever it is, be sure the spark is there for you. Don't settle for anything less.

Accepting that as the most basic guideline, what next? Let's hope that there are several stories or parts of stories that excite you. Now it's time to look at them more critically. Ask yourself which ones have potential for action onstage. The story itself may not have been told in a way that emphasized action, or the action it used might be difficult to do onstage. This may not matter; think beyond the specifics of the story to the idea behind it. Can the theme of the piece be told in terms of action? Can the characters be *doing* things to get what they want and not just talking about them and thinking about them?

If everything happens in their minds, the story is not going to adapt well to stage. Fantasies, daydreams, and remembrances of the past can be acted out, however, and it's possible that events only referred to by characters in a story might be performed in a play version in a way that moves the tale forward.

In addition to potential for action, does the story have appealing characters? Do you care about them? The appeal might be because they are sympathetic and you identify with them. It might be because they are infuriating! You want an interesting mix of people, and the main person, of course, needs to be someone you like. The character doesn't have to be perfect or strong or terribly brave or popular, but he or she must be someone you and the audience will care about. Then there are the others who are helpful or not helpful to your main character.

Characters need not be human, by the way. They can be animals, fantasy creatures, or objects. You might like a story in which colors are the main characters, or a candy bar and a vending machine. Such characters represent people, for all plays are really about what people feel and do in the world. A story might be told in terms of animals in order to give them single, bold qualities. A mouse outsmarting a lion, for instance, puts more emphasis on the

8

difference in the characters' size and strength than you'd get telling your trickster tale in terms of a small boy outsmarting a large, angry principal. Of course, if your story needs a realistic school setting, create the characters as humans, but you might keep the image of the animals in the back of your mind as you write their **lines.**

When we turn animals or objects into characters, we are anthropomorphizing them—that is, giving them human characteristics. Our stories about them are really about ourselves as humans. Don't think that a good story about a hard rubber ball and a sagging beach ball or one about a rock and a tree won't make good plays. To dramatize either of them, you could have actors behave as people who have qualities like a ball or a tree, or you could indicate in your **stage directions** that the actors should dress and act as much like a ball or a tree as possible. Another approach would be to treat a real ball or a small tree like a puppet and move it as a puppeteer would, speaking for the object. Remember that a character needs to do things, even a character that is a picture hanging on a wall or someone sick in bed. A play is interesting only when characters make things happen around them.

Given the initial spark, potential for action, and appealing characters, it's time now to see whether or not a story's idea or theme is one that you feel is important and worth sharing with others. Even though you might like a character in the story or find some of the action very funny, the total piece may be saying something about people and life that you disagree with. Stop to consider the message. You want it to be one you share and wish to share with others. If it isn't, perhaps there is another way you could treat the characters and the plot line to give it the emphasis you want. If you choose to do this, however, you must make it clear on your title page and on the program for the **production** of the play that this script is *your* version of the original. Many writers take plots or characters from existing stories and interpret them in their own way. Shakespeare, one of the greatest playwrights in the English language, rarely made up plots from scratch; he borrowed characters and plots from stories and other plays, or from history, and turned them into plays that were uniquely his and said what he wanted to say about life.

If none of your stories seem right after you've looked at them with these points in mind, look further and keep reading. Ask a librarian to suggest a variety of books. Classics in literature and Biblical stories are often dramatized. Norse and Greek myths, as well as folktales such as the Anansi tales from West Africa, the Raven tales from Northwestern Native Americans, Juan Bobo stories from Latin America, and the Monkey King stories from China provide endless choices. There are many modern stories, too, but remember that most of these are protected by copyright and may be dramatized only with permission of the author. (Write to him or her in care of the publisher of the book in which you found it.)

It is usually easier to dramatize folktales than fairy tales or myths, both of which involve the supernatural. The kinds of powers possessed by fairies, witches, ogres, or gods are difficult for people to portray. Of course, you don't need to make someone really fly through the air, as a big professional production of *Peter Pan* might do. You can use expressive movement by actors that the audience will accept as flying, or casting spells, or turning oneself into a cricket. But even creating simple solutions to the problem of showing magical powers leaves you with the basic problem of creating a believable world on stage that is different from the human world.

Folktales, on the other hand, usually deal with people in the real world. Even if the characters are animals (who stand for people), the kinds of things they do are of our day-to-day world rather than of our dreams and fantasies. Another advantage of folktales is that they were created to teach lessons about life, and they had to be interesting and fun or people wouldn't listen. Only the best have lasted hundreds of years. They have been tested by time and usually appeal to a lot of people.

Look in magazines for stories. Check out newspapers. Your own imagination can turn a news item into a full story. An insightful writer, E.M. Forester, once illustrated the difference between factual news and a story with the following two sentences: "The King died and the Queen died," and "The King died, and the Queen died of grief." You can readily sense the difference. The first feels cold and abbreviated. It is straight reporting. The second, though short, involves feelings, cause and effect. Can you read between the lines of a news item and imagine the full story?

Then there are stories you have heard, tales a relative told you, or old folktales that weren't written down. Funny or strange things that happened to someone in the family might have been repeated for years. A friend might have told you something that happened to someone he or she knew. Or maybe it happened to you! Can you be so proper that nothing crazy ever happened to you? Are you so perfect that you never made an embarrassing mistake? Were you ever punished for something you didn't do? All such stuff of our lives could make a play or become part of a play.

11

Dreams and daydreams or fantasies are wonderful sources for stories. When these fantasies are your own, they are often easier to work with than the ancient fantasies or myths that you may not understand. They are wonderful because the world isn't just what we see before us any more than our lives are just what appears on the outside. Underneath every action and object are layers of things imagined, wished for, felt, dreamed of. It is said that dreams are our way of digesting things we experience during our waking hours. We need time for dreaming just as we need time to digest food. What better source for a play than a dream, particularly a very strong one that is riveted in your mind, one that woke you up in a sweat or continues to reappear? The simple experiences of life are ones we don't need to make plays about. We're more interested in experiences that need some work to understand or accept. The understanding doesn't have to be somber, either. Laughter does wonders in helping us see something we've avoided or accept something pushed aside or something that no longer fits us.

You can dream up a story while you're awake, too. No one ever reprimanded a storyteller or playwright with "Stop daydreaming!" or "You only made that up." Only made it up? What could be nicer! I hope you make up lots of tales—fantastic ones, funny ones, sad ones, wild ones. Practice regularly on your friends, on your family. If they are sticklers for the truth, tell them at the outset or at the end that the story was your own, but don't put down your creation or yourself by saying, "It was *only* a story." Instead, try saying, "I have a great story for you!"

⁘3⁘

Getting Started on Your Script: The First Draft

There are many ways of going about writing a script. Don't get trapped into thinking there's one proper way or that there's only one way that works for you. Surprise yourself. Nothing is worse than being stuck with a piece of blank paper staring at you and no ideas coming or general ideas swimming around with no handle by which to hold on to them. It often helps me to have a group of actors **improvise** some scenes to give me an idea of how it might go, but some people prefer to work quietly on their own, writing a script before having actors try it. Sometimes you want to get going on a project when there aren't any people around to act things out, so it's necessary to see everything in your imagination. **Collaborating,** or working with, one or two other writers is another effective way of getting started. One person's idea will spark someone, and you're off. How about talking into a tape recorder, taking on the voices of the various characters? What about drawing key scenes or making simple comic-book-type sketches with stick figures going through a series of events?

Whatever method you use, it is helpful first to go over

13

your story carefully and become thoroughly familiar with the sequence of events, the characters, the various locations, and other details. *List the main events.* You might make little branches off the main line to record supporting events or subplots. List the places involved so you can be thinking about *locale.* And, of course, list the *characters.* You'll want to underline or star the most important ones. All stories have a few key characters, without whom the story wouldn't exist, and then there are often minor characters who add color to the plot but aren't essential to it. If you can distinguish between principal characters and **supporting characters** it will be easier for you to know how to expand or contract the total number of characters if you need to adjust the size of the cast for a particular group of actors.

When you're quite familiar with the feeling of the story as a whole and its elements (the characters, the main events, the locations used), then put the story aside and deal with the parts themselves rather than continuing to think about how the story was told in its original version. Decide how you would like your play to start on stage. Where shall the first scene take place? How do you want to introduce the characters and the situation? What are some of the important scenes to follow? Make some initial decisions about how many scenes you'll use, where they will take place, who is in them, and what happens in each. Each scene must give us new information and move the action forward toward the ending, and it is usually more dramatic and effective if either the situation or the characters change in some way during that scene. It's more exciting if each scene ends in such a way that the audience is eager to know what will happen next.

14

Try a rough draft, either in writing or by having actors improvise it. Have a look at what you've got. You'll be very surprised and pleased with some things that appear on their own, as though you'd had no hand in it, and with other things you had doubts about that turn out to be very effective. Then there'll be parts that don't work at all. Try to see or read what's in front of you with an open mind. It's unlikely that it will all be wonderful and just the way you want it. Don't be discouraged! It's also quite unlikely that all of it is terrible and not worth keeping. See if you (and any others working with you as actors, audience, readers, advisors) can *first focus on aspects of the work that genuinely please you.* It may be the way a particular character came across in the writing or the acting. It may be the way two characters interacted with each other. It may be the way the actors used their bodies to create a sense of the location and not at all what the characters were saying.

Playwriting isn't just about giving characters things to say; it is about setting up a series of situations in which characters act and react. What they actually say is the icing on the cake. You and the actors first have to figure out what the characters want and how they're going to go about getting it. Then the words will come. Therefore, in evaluating the work (whether it's written or acted), note any aspect of it that is pleasing to you, whether it has to do with the lines or not. *Keep a record* of what you like either with written notes or by recording on tape.

Now look objectively at the parts that were weak. See if you can figure out why they didn't work. Boring? Confusing? Inappropriately funny? Perhaps the actors, or you as writer, were unclear about what a character was doing in a particular scene. Perhaps there was too much going on at once for the audience to follow the action. Maybe not enough was happening; the characters were just standing around talking. Remember, characters have to do things to bring them closer to their goal. When you look at the first draft for its strong points and weak points, several ideas for changes will undoubtedly occur to you. That's enough to work with, even if you can't figure out solutions to all the problems.

By the way, it isn't necessary to write or improvise a draft of the whole story before you begin to evaluate and rework it. Perhaps at the outset you can't figure out how many scenes you want to use to tell the whole story. Just start with the parts that are clear to you. Once you're into it, other ideas will come, and you'll take courage from seeing how some of it works very nicely.

Now do another draft of the whole or the scenes you're working on. But if you're working on parts of the play rather than the whole, don't try more than one revision of any of the parts until you have tried a rough draft of everything. Your ideas about the various sections will be affected by how the pieces work together, so it isn't wise to refine any one section in isolation from the rest. A sculptor wouldn't finish the arm or leg of a statue without shaping the whole piece first. Usually an artist keeps moving over the entire piece as he or she refines the work so that its parts develop together. And remember that most artists do several revisions of their rough draft before reaching a version they feel satisfied with.

16

❍❍❍ 4 ❍❍❍

Artistic Considerations: Questions to Ask When Evaluating Your Script

There are two types of questions to ask yourself when you **critique** or evaluate your drafts. One type is artistic or aesthetic questions. These are considerations basic to the art form in which you are working—in this case, playwriting. The other type is questions of a practical nature. They are of equal importance because they involve the real issues of your particular set of circumstances. It doesn't matter which you consider first; you may prefer to juggle back and forth between the two. I have decided to discuss the artistic ones first, but you are invited to jump ahead to Chapter Five if you wish to start with the practical.

A key question for any play is: *What is it about?* Can you simply state the main issue of your play? For instance, *Peter Pan* is about not wanting to grow up and leave the fantasies of childhood. *The Wizard of Oz* is about learning to love your friends and home. This sounds simple, but it isn't always. Sometimes it's very tricky to identify what a story is about or what you want to say with your play, and you

17

won't find agreement among all people. I'm sure you'll find people who disagree with my statements about *Peter Pan* and *The Wizard of Oz*. What is important is that you decide what *you* want the main issue of the play to be. There may also be secondary issues that support the main one and give it levels of meaning. For instance, in *Peter Pan* a secondary issue is the power of friendship and loyalty to one's friends. It's fine to have secondary theses, but it's important that you are clear about the primary one as you develop your script.

Another key question to ask is: *Whose story is it?* Many plays have fallen apart in the writing or the directing because the playwright or the **director** wasn't clear about whose story the play was. Don't let the title fool you. *The Wizard of Oz* is not the Wizard's tale. It is Dorothy's. On the other hand, *Peter Pan* is Peter's story and not Wendy's, John's, or Michael's, even though they are the first important characters introduced in the play. Often a story can be interpreted in more than one way. You could take a well-known tale like *Goldilocks and the Three Bears*, for instance, and make it either Goldilocks' story or the three bears' story. Some versions of the story place emphasis on the girl and some on the bears. In choosing, you have to decide what you want to say about people and the world before knowing whom to make the principal characters. Then let us see the events as they relate to that character. It is possible, by the way, to have more than one character serve as the principal character, but this approach works only if they act as a unit. We need to see them as a constant group rather than as people with distinctly different personalities. The comic team the Three Stooges is an example of

18

characters treated this way. Those wacky characters have slightly different qualities, but they share their strongest one: their way of entering any situation and causing an uproar. The three are always the principal characters in scripts about their experiences, no matter how many other interesting people are involved in the situation.

In addition to identifying the main character, *have you made the other characters clear?* Are there enough differences among them to enable the audience to recognize them as separate people? And are these separate people consistent throughout the play? Naturally any character will behave differently in different situations and may undergo change during the play, but when you look at each one from beginning through to the end, he or she should be believable as the same person. This is true whether you are using realistic people as characters or wildly fantastic creatures.

Does the total group of characters in your play create *an interesting balance of types*? It may be that two or three of them are very similar in personality although you hadn't intended that effect. If so, see how you might alter some of them. If the original story doesn't give you any clues, look at people around you in school, at home, at church or temple, in the neighborhood, in other books to get some ideas. If the characters are animals, for instance, in addition to studying a real animal of that type for movement and personality ideas, you might use people to give you an interesting image for your animal. Your dog character might behave something like the policewoman at your school crossing, or your horse character might behave like an uncle of yours.

Suppose you want a group of characters to be quite similar, such as a group of townspeople or a herd of goats. You may want the bizarre effect of having them behave identically, but it's more likely you'd be less extreme and have each one become a slight variation on the theme the group represents. Say the overall effect you want is that of timid characters. One could try to hide behind another; one could nervously repeat other characters' words in agreement; one could laugh self-consciously; one could frequently say, "Oh, I don't know; don't ask me!"

Let your actors help create the characters if you can work with **improvisation** to create your play. It's a lot of fun to find distinctive physical movements and voices, complete personalities, an unusual rhythm and tempo of moving and speaking. It's helpful when the actors and the director share in this process.

Another big question is: *Are the ideas of the play told through action or through talking?* If Anansi, the trickster spider, wants to fool some characters, don't have him talk about how he is going to do this; it's more fun for us to see him in the process of setting up the trick and pulling it off or being caught in it. If you want to establish the fact that a character in your play is well-liked because she often does thoughtful things for others, set up a few situations in which we can see the character doing favors, lending a helping hand. It's usually more effective to see her help a person put spilled groceries back into a bag and see the old man thank her and comment to his companion that he was pleased by her helpfulness than to have someone tell you she did this. This does not mean that it's never appropriate to let characters describe things that happened or comment on other characters' behavior, but check through your play to see that the balance of talking and action pleases you. Usually we want to see people doing things rather than talking about them. The doing and the action doesn't always have to be physically active. The doing might be helping a friend by talking to him about why he feels so sad about leaving. Or it could be a person laid up with a broken leg being perfectly obnoxious by bossing everyone around. Remember that in a play, action is what the characters do to get them what they want, to bring them closer to their goal.

Is there a beginning, a middle, and an end to your play? Ask yourself again what the play is about. Then ask how the whole story begins. A story that's told or read usually begins differently from the opening of a play. Of course, if you are doing what is called Story Theater, you would have a narrator or the characters introducing the play in story form and linking parts of the action with story narrative. For instance, a narrator or one of the characters might say, "Once upon a time in a little hut, on the edge of a deep forest, there lived a little girl . . ." and the characters enter and begin the action. Sometimes the narrator continues telling and describing the action. Often the characters take over with **dialogue.** Sometimes characters switch back and forth between speaking as storyteller and then as a character in the action.

But, unless you're doing Story Theater, you must think how you will introduce the situation of a character like Little Red Riding Hood living alone with her mother near the woods, a carefree, innocent girl who enjoys life around her. Or perhaps in your version you want to make her a selfish, annoying little brat. Have the characters do things that will establish what you want the audience to know about the situation. Then have the first piece of action begin: Little Red's mother asks her to take a basket of goodies to Grandmother who is sick in bed in her house on the other side of the woods. The middle part of the play consists of all the pieces of action that lead up to the most exciting moment: is Little Red going to realize that "Grandmother" is the Wolf in disguise in time to save herself from being eaten? The middle part should lead up to this high point of **crisis.** You can put in all kinds of action leading up to this, including some side issues, songs, and dances, but they mustn't stop the action from moving along. You want to build our interest to the point of crisis. Then give us an ending that is clear and happens fairly quickly so we feel the danger is over and we all know what happens to Little Red. The ending may be happy or unhappy, but we need to know what the outcome is, how the main character fared in her quest or objective in the play. For Little Red Riding Hood, it would be most important to let us know how Little Red makes out in her goal of delivering the food to Grandma. We also want to know the outcome for the other important characters. What happens to the Wolf? Is he killed or punished? What happens to Grandma? Does she die when eaten? Does she escape in the end? It's all right to decide to leave us with a few questions, such as whether or not Little Red will ever venture into the woods alone again, or you can end your tale with all the questions answered. That's your choice as an interpreter of the story.

A final question to ask yourself at this point in evaluating your draft is: *Does your play have a point of view?* If you are writing a script based on Little Red Riding Hood, the chances are that most of the people in your audience will have heard of this story before seeing or reading your play. Since the plot is not new, why are you doing it? You don't have to think of a new twist or a new ending, but you do have to have a point of view about the story so that the people watching the play will know what you think this story is saying about people and the world. Is it: Always be on guard because you never know what dangers are out there in the world? Is it: Despite the scary things that exist in the world, if you are kind, helpful, and trusting, help will be there when you need it? These are only two interpretations; many others are possible. But even considering only these two, you can see that your script would have to be different if you wished to make the first point rather than the second. The point of view does not have to be as obvious as it would be in the treatment of a fable, a short teaching tale, where the moral is actually stated at the end, such as, "Don't cry over spilt milk." And it doesn't have to be so obvious that there are no questions left in the minds of the audience. You do want them to think about the play and discuss it with others afterward. All good plays are open to interpretation in a variety of ways, but as the playwright, you need to know what you want to say so that all parts of the script effectively contribute to this statement.

$\bullet\bullet\bullet 5 \bullet\bullet\bullet$

Practical Considerations: Adapting to Special Circumstances

Sometimes you start on a theater project without realizing what goals you have in the back of your mind, or sometimes you start out with clear goals and then change them in the course of working on the project. It might help to identify three popular theater activities that have very different goals.

Creative drama is one; it's the term we use for acting things out for the fun of it. Scripts are not involved because people make up their own lines as they act. Audiences are not involved, except for members of the group who usually alternate between watching and acting. Scenes are not usually repeated because a new situation is created for each new team. Creative drama is a wonderful way to develop ideas, build acting skills, and have fun.

Production work is theater work prepared for an audience, and its goal is to present a performance. People may work from a script to do this or they may improvise their lines. The scenes are usually repeated many times in

rehearsal because the actors and director want to shape the piece in a particular way. It can also help build acting skills and can be a lot of fun; it's important to keep it this way and not let the tension about performing for an audience turn it into an unpleasant situation.

Playwriting is making up a plan for a play; it usually involves writing a script for a play that can be used again and again by different performers. Playwriting can be done by one person writing alone, by a team of writers, or by a whole group acting out scenes together and later writing them down. It can be done with a particular production in mind or with no immediate production planned, but rather to give form to an idea in the writer's head.

Organizing people to produce a play—in other words, preparing it for an audience—is a lot of work. It is difficult and can be frustrating as well as exciting. It may be more than you want to take on at the same time you are writing your play. If so, see the play in your mind's eye as you write and put your energy into finishing the script. Let someone else at another time (maybe you) deal with the task of directing a production for performance.

Casting Issues

If you are writing your play without a specific theater production in mind, you are free to pick the number of characters that you feel will be most effective for telling the tale. That might be the number of characters in the original story or it could be the way you visualize that story when it comes alive in your imagination. *The Three Billy Goats Gruff* could be done with three goats and a troll, or a whole field of goats, of which only three are spunky enough to take action about the lack of grass in their field, and a great monstrous troll made of three or four actors. You can suggest alternate ways of casting your script to give directors different ideas for using it. If you're not sure what the best number of characters would be and you do not have a group of actors with whom to try out the scenes, concentrate hard to imagine the scenes in action. Do they seem thin? Do they feel crowded or confusing with too many people? Does the number of people balance well? It's usually best not to have a character appear only momentarily to provide a piece of information; see if you can find ways to do without such a character or find reasons to use him or her elsewhere. If the story absolutely needs to have someone appear only once for a brief exchange, try to use a few other such characters elsewhere in the play. Create a balance so the one won't stand out as being quite different from the other characters.

Often when you are adapting a story to play form, you are thinking of a particular production. If this is the case, keep your special circumstances in mind as you evaluate your draft of the script and adjust it accordingly. Suppose you know you'll have only a *very few actors*. You might then select a story with only a few characters. However, there are other solutions. A small ensemble of five actors could play many different roles by changing their costumes and the way they use their voices and bodies. If you want the effect to be fairly realistic, write the scenes so that no more than your total number of actors are ever onstage at the same time and there's enough time between scenes for people to change costumes. Use a musical interlude or have some characters exit earlier than others so the actors playing them can change and be ready to start the next scene as new characters. If you want to be very public about using a small ensemble of actors, you can introduce your company of actors at the beginning, having them wear neutral or basic costumes, and then, as they assume the various roles, let them change parts of their costumes in view of the audience. An even more stylized way of working would be to have the actors hold masks on sticks in front of their faces as they speak and change masks for each character they assume. An actor might even use a row of connected face masks or body masks to represent a whole group of people such as policemen answering a call for help, an audience of concertgoers, sports fans watching a tennis game.

Perhaps your special circumstances are that you have *many actors* wanting roles in the play. Think how you might expand the number of characters called for by the original story. In the case of the folktale *Stone Soup*, add more townspeople for the hungry soldier to ask for food; create many types of people with excuses for not helping. Some of these people might have animals with them, such as a dog, a cow, a flock of geese, all of which can be played by actors. In the folktale *The Bojabi Tree* the village of animals could be comprised of many in addition to the Rat, Pig, Goat, and Turtle who volunteer to go up the river to visit Lion. The river might be made by people moving strips of cloth or painted cardboard or actually be formed by moving people. Lion could have a wife and some children. A group of actors could form the Bojabi tree. A story like *Emil and the Detectives* by Erich Kastner that takes place in a city might have actors being buildings or cars or pedestrians on the sidewalk. Another approach for using more actors would be to select several short tales that seem to fit together because of their theme or because they are all from one culture. Present them as a series, connected by some theatrical device, such as a musical or dance interlude, and have a different cast of actors for each tale.

Perhaps none of these solutions will work for you without pulling your script out of shape. Don't fight it, then. Use the script as it is and find other ways to use the eager actors. Perhaps the director would be willing to direct two casts to perform at alternate times. The extra actors might be willing to work on a piece of their own, such as a dance, some songs, or some instrumental music, to accompany your play. Or they could become the crew and make the sets, costumes, sound effects, programs, and posters and wait for their turn at acting till the next production.

Your special casting circumstances might not be the number of actors you have but the fact that they are *unsure of themselves onstage.* Help them by putting more emphasis in your script on group scenes. Keep the exchanges between two and three characters fairly short and use other characters to back them up whenever appropriate. It is hard for inexperienced actors to do long scenes between two or three people. Give them interaction among many people and create reasons for the characters to be doing things as they talk, so the actors can be engaged in **stage business** and not find themselves standing around self-consciously. If you are especially careful to make clear what each character wants in the whole play as well as in each scene, it will make the job of acting easier for the actors, whether they are strong or weak.

28

Production Issues

Suppose you know when you're writing that there'll be *no budget or technical help* for the production of your play. This means you won't have money to spend for sets, costumes, or props, and there'll be no people to help you prepare sets or costumes. You aren't the first person who has been in this situation. Don't let it stop you from doing your play. Focus on what you and the actors can do by yourselves to bring the play to life. Leave out spectacular theatrical effects and create situations that the actors can pull off with their acting alone. Make the exchanges between characters important. Emphasize movement. Let actors use their bodies to create effects of scenery either as characters responding to the imagined environment or by becoming the scenery. Find a place to perform that has an uncluttered background, curtains you could pull, or screens you could set up. Ask the cast to use clothing they own that could be appropriate for their characters. You can make the actors' own clothes look like costumes by using a basic outfit like jeans or sweat pants for everyone and adding just a few specific pieces like a hat or scarf or apron appropriate for the various characters. When you have just a few design elements, keep them simple and choose them carefully so that the production will be as unified and uncluttered as possible.

Suppose, on the other hand, you have *lots of eager people to help construct sets, costumes, props, and even masks.* By all means use them, but talk with these people often to be sure you're all working toward the same goal. Insist that the technical things be ready well in advance of the performance date to give the actors plenty of time to practice using them. It takes more than a couple of rehearsals to get used to a costume or the set, and use of masks requires an even longer rehearsal period.

If you are planning a complicated production, make your task simpler. Get someone to help you by becoming **producer.** The producer is responsible for seeing that all contributions—the rehearsed play, the scenery, the costumes, lights, sound, and publicity—come together to assure an audience for your performance.

Another condition may be that you have *no director* to help you and the actors prepare your production. Then work closely with the actors yourself so that you and they are clear about the effect you all want from the script. If you find that they often are unable to bring the scenes to life the way you intended, you may have to rewrite some of the scenes, making them less complicated so that the actors will have an easier time of it. Long speeches that involve little action are difficult. Break these up with more exchanges among characters. Highly emotional scenes where a person cries or reveals to another character that he or she loves that person are usually hard for inexperienced actors to perform; they don't know how to bring up such intense feeling on cue or they feel embarrassed to show it. If you don't have someone who knows how to coach them on this, you can help by making the statements about feelings as simple and direct as possible. For instance, change "I love you, darling; you mean everything to me" to "I like you a lot, Fredo; I feel you're my best friend." How you simplify a line, of course, depends completely on the situation that exists in your play. Think of how those particular people

30

would talk rather than how you've heard it done in films or television shows you've seen. It often works well to have the actor playing the part come up with the words that he or she feels most comfortable saying.

If your actors are truly shy and *unable to speak up* in front of an audience, you might consider keeping your script very close to story form and use a narrator (as in Story Theater) or even some speaking actors at one side of the stage telling the story while others go through the action onstage. This approach can be particularly effective if there are interesting sets and costumes for the audience to look at. Some performers feel freer without words to speak; they will create expressive movement and action to bring the piece to life. The more effective they can be, the less the narrator will have to fill in with the storytelling. It helps to give the narrator exciting and descriptive words that will stimulate the imagination of both the actors and the audience.

Relationship of Your Script to the Original Story

Be clear for yourself and your audience about how close you want to stay to the original story if it has been written by someone other than yourself. It will help you make decisions about how to treat your play version. On the title page of your script (and later on the poster and program), let the reader know what the relationship will be to help avoid misunderstandings.

A *dramatization* of the story is a play version that closely follows the plot, the number of characters, and the style and tone of the original source. When you want to be true to the original, you'll probably return to it fairly often to refresh your thinking about its tone and details.

If you are doing an *adaptation* from the story to dramatic form, however, you have more freedom to alter aspects of the story to make it work as theater. You might change sequences of events, alter characters, omit sections.

When you only base your script on a story, you have considerable leeway in rearranging, adding to, and eliminating elements of the original. *Based on* implies that you are only using the story as a starting point but are not attempting to dramatize all aspects of it.

You can give yourself even more freedom by stating that your script is only *loosely based on* the story. In such cases, it lets the audience know that the original was a source of inspiration to you but that they should not expect to see the story they know.

These distinctions may seem unimportant, but you want to avoid misleading your reader or your audience. You will often find that when you are working with a well-known and well-loved story or with an unusual story that a few people know and are pleased to discover that you have chosen to work with, these people will become upset if your stage version of the piece is different from what they expected. If you can let them know at the outset whether or not you'll be sticking closely to the original, they won't be looking for something you do not intend to give them. It is to your advantage to put your audience in the most receptive frame of mind with which to receive your play.

Visualizing the Production

Sometimes you write a script knowing the specific production conditions in which it will be used; sometimes you write without a performance occasion ready but hoping to inspire others to do a production of your play. Whatever the circumstances, try to visualize the play in action as you are creating your script. Let this come through in the dialogue you write as well as in the stage directions. You might even want to address notes to the actors and director describing how particular effects could be achieved. Naturally it will be easier for people producing your script if you are moderate rather than elaborate in the number of characters and scenes you call for, as well as in the special technical effects your play requires. Think it through carefully. Probably more people will want to use a script that is not too demanding. On the other hand, as an artist you are perfectly free to invent a fantastic vision that will challenge creative minds to match your script with an equally fantastic production. An example of this is Ruth Krauss, who wrote some unusual plays that stretch the imagination. One of them starts with the stage direction: "1500 horses rush by going East; 1500 horses rush by going West." An exciting production of these short, fanciful plays was done by an equally imaginative director, Remy Charlip, who enjoyed the challenge of staging this unusual image. There is no virtue in being big or small, elaborate or simple with your script. Good plays, exciting plays, funny plays, moving plays have been written in all sizes with all levels of complication. The important issue is whether or not you are able to capture through the writing of your script your excitement about your vision of the play. This vision will then inspire performing artists to contribute their part to bring the play alive.

6

Fine Tuning:
The Form of a Play

After you've evaluated your draft, made changes, and looked at it again, you may feel well satisfied with the result—or you may feel not completely satisfied, but as though you've invested as much time and effort as you want to on this venture. However, if you are aware that some parts are not working just right and you're eager to make the most effective script possible, take courage and look at it again. Most writers have to write and rewrite their plays many times before getting them the way they want them. Don't think it's because you're a beginner that you have to make so many changes. In fact, it's the other way around: it's usually the experienced people who have more patience to do rewriting to shape the script the way they want it.

You might return to Chapter Four, Artistic Considerations: Questions to Ask When Evaluating Your Draft. If those questions help you identify more changes that could help, continue to work with that approach. You may also find it helpful to read this chapter, which is more technical in its discussion of dramatic form.

The Premise of Your Play

A play needs a **premise** or main issue. Whatever the style or form of your play—comic, serious, musical, traditional, experimental—it will be more effective if it has a central idea that you can state clearly for yourself. All the elements of the play should work in some way to make this main issue clear. Sometimes you don't really know what this basic issue is until after you have worked on the play for some time. Creative work doesn't move ahead logically. Writing a play isn't like writing a book report or an essay. Often you start with only a character, a hunch, or a feeling, instead of an idea. Moreover, when you turn a story into a play, the story you selected may have interested you for a reason you can not yet describe even to yourself. This needn't stop you from starting to work on your play. But once you are at the stage of revising a draft of the play, you must ask some questions about what you are really saying with it (in other words, its premise or main idea) and how you are saying it (in other words, its form). And you will need to begin to find answers.

The Form of A Play

As you read the following section on structure or dramatic form, see if you can identify the elements discussed here in your script. The classical or traditional form for writing plays is the one most often used in turning stories into plays. Not all plays are written in this form, but it is the most familiar one to us in the Western world. It is used for many film and television scripts as well as stage plays. It is the form described in the rest of this chapter.

Use of Characters

Basic to a traditional script is the existence of a main character. Sometimes this person is called the primary character or the **protagonist;** he or she is the mover of the piece. It is the person whose story the play is; it is the person who sets things into motion; it is the person about whom we are the most concerned. In *Annie* it would be Little Orphan Annie; in *The Sound of Music* it would be Maria; in *West Side Story,* Tony; in a play about Peter Rabbit it would be Peter.

Then there is a secondary character with whom the protagonist has an important relationship. In *West Side Story* it would be Maria; in the *Tale of Peter Rabbit* it would be Peter's mother. Our main character may be trying to get closer to this secondary character, as Tony does to Maria, or to gain some independence from this secondary character, as Peter does from his mother. In *Annie* the secondary character would be Daddy Warbucks, the parent Annie is trying to find; in *The Sound of Music* it would be Captain von Trapp, whom Maria learns to love.

A third character comes into the situation to jar our main characters; this character is usually called the **antagonist.** The antagonist keeps events from moving smoothly along, thereby creating the drama of the piece. If Annie did not have a nasty Miss Hannigan at the orphanage trying to take money from the kids living there, if Peter did not encounter Mr. McGregor, if Tony was not threatened by the hostility of Bernardo, leader of the Sharks, the stories of these characters would not haunt us the way they do. It is the fact that the main characters do not have an easy time doing what they want to do that draws us into their lives and involves us with their struggle.

A play can certainly have more than just these three characters: the protagonist, the secondary character, and the antagonist. Extra characters are often important in filling out the story. They can reinforce the action of any one of the three principals. The Sharks make Bernardo's threat as antagonist even stronger; the many orphans in Annie's home make Annie's search for her parents even more urgent. Sometimes in a complicated play like Shakespeare's *King Lear,* the main issue of the piece—the king's search for love from his three daughters and his loss of power—is made more moving by a parallel situation. In this case it is the subplot involving King Lear's counselor Gloucester and Gloucester's relationship with his two sons.

A play might have only one or two characters. When this is the case, the relationship of the secondary character and antagonist is implied. This can be done by repeated mention of the missing person. In a two-person piece, the antagonist could be a threatening person from the past, the memory of whom creates the problems between the two. Or perhaps the two characters onstage are protagonist and antagonist and it is the secondary character who exists in their awareness only. For instance, in a play about a kidnapped child, if the kidnapper is the antagonist and the child is the protagonist, the secondary character might be her father whom she is trying to rejoin and to whom the kidnapper is sending ransom notes. An object in the scene with two characters could serve as the secondary character: a bench that two men want to sit on alone can take on a force of its own, as in *The Zoo Story* by Edward Albee. Objects often serve as characters when you have a play with only one character: Charlie Chaplin, the silent film star, made many little scenes involving comic exchanges between his character and the objects he came into contact with. Another device is to have the character's younger self become one of the characters to whom the main character talks. And, of course, the single-character can talk to other people in his or her mind, bringing them onto the stage one or several at a time. It is hard to create a long, complicated play this way, however; a single-character play is more likely to be a short **sketch.**

Regardless of the number of characters in your play, it is important to be clear about the main issue. Don't let any of the characters become too brief or too important for the function they serve in the whole script. You may have to cut back some characters you really like if they take our attention away from the main thrust of the action. Likewise, you may have to work hard to create more interesting things for the main character to say and do if this person isn't developed enough to hold our interest.

Plot

In a traditional play, the plot of your script needs a particular shape. The plot is the series of events that occur. It deals with the action of the play. Closely related to it, of course, are the feelings of the characters that prompt the action or result from the action. The **opening** of the play sets up the situation in which the action of the play occurs. This opening is sometimes called the **exposition.** With it, in as interesting a way as possible, you need to let the audience know where we are, what has been going on up to now, and some of the main characters involved. The way in which you set this up will also let us know if the play is to be funny, serious, a fantasy, a mystery, a musical. The opening indicates the style and tone of the piece; for a play it is the theatrical way of presenting the once-upon-a-time opening used in a story. Try to introduce the main elements you plan to use in your play during this exposition, so that although we certainly may be surprised later on, we won't be jolted. For instance, if you plan to use a narrator or music or have the whole piece done silently in mime, let the opening reflect this style.

The **beginning action** of the play occurs when something happens to upset the situation you established in the opening. This is when the drama starts. In *The Tale of Peter Rabbit,* it would be after Mother Rabbit dresses Peter and sends him out to play, warning him not to go near Mr. McGregor's vegetable garden, and *Peter decides to go.* Up to that point you have learned that this is to be a play about rabbits, that home is a safe place for them, and that there is a dangerous place that Mother warns her son to stay away from. This is important information for the drama, but no drama occurs in *The Tale of Peter Rabbit* until the main character decides to do something that is forbidden and that might upset the peace and quiet of his life. Because this decision makes all the difference, be sure that your script makes this moment clear. Don't have Peter just sort of end up in the garden. He can charge out to get there; he can sneak up on it; he can accidentally-on-purpose end up at the edge of it and decide to enter because he is so close. There are any number of ways to get him to go there, and the one you choose will reflect the kind of character you are creating in your script. Don't throw away this important beginning moment of the play.

In *West Side Story* the beginning moment is when Tony sees Maria at the dance and falls in love with her, knowing she's from the rival group. In *The Sound of Music* it's when Maria accepts the job of governess and goes to the von Trapp home. In *Annie* it's when Annie tells the kids that she has a memento from her real parents that's going to help her find them. The fact that she's one of many orphans in an orphanage doesn't create drama. The fact that one particular orphan is determined to locate her real parents creates the beginning of one. This beginning action upsets the opening situation.

Once the action has begun, there need to be **developments** that lead from one event into the next. This is where the feelings are related to the action. Annie is offered the chance to go with some people who want to adopt her, but, because she wants very much to find her own parents, she does not accept this as her final home and remains determined to locate her real parents. Because Peter is a curious and adventuresome rabbit, he decides to go into the forbidden garden, and, having made this bold move, he becomes more daring and takes things from under Mr. McGregor's nose. His daring makes him less cautious, so that he walks right into the cat. You see how one piece of action leads to the next with cause and effect. The events are not random.

Although there may be unexpected surprises, each set of actions gives rise to the next round.

The series of events lead to a crisis. In a short play there might be only one main piece of action before the protagonist finds herself or himself in a crisis. In a long play, of course, many events may occur before that point. But few or many, in a traditional play we need a situation of crisis in which the main character is caught between two forces and must make a decision to go one way or the other. This decision will change the course of events. The main character needs to make this decision because the play is his or her story. The drama will not be satisfying if someone other than the protagonist makes the choice. Peter meets Mr. McGregor face to face and runs for his life. Annie accepts the fact that her parents no longer exist and decides to accept Daddy Warbucks for her adoptive father. Maria decides to not run away from her feelings of love and returns to Captain von Trapp's house to talk with him of her love. Tony decides to find Maria even though he knows one of the Sharks has sworn to kill him. All the events of the play need to lead up to this moment of high tension. Even in a comedy this moment is tense, although the situation may be funny. Previous moments can involve tension as well; there may be a series of smaller crises leading up to the final one. But the main crisis is the one in which you ask the most basic question of the play: Will Peter's curiosity cost him his life? Will Tony be united with Maria despite the gang war surrounding them? Will Annie find the parents she wants? Will Maria be able to break through the traditions of the church and the social class structure to be united with Captain von Trapp?

The **climax** is the high point of the play, coming immediately after the moment in the crisis when the main character makes the important decision facing him or her. The climax is what follows as a result of this decision; it is the most emotional point of the play because here we see the main question of the play being answered. Peter runs for his life and manages barely to escape Mr. McGregor, losing his clothes in the process. Tony finds Maria but is shot to death just as he runs to meet her. Annie accepts Daddy Warbucks and is able to leave the orphanage forever. Maria marries Captain von Trapp and joins her efforts with his to save the children and themselves from the Nazis.

Even though the question of the play is answered when the climax is over, there is still a last part needed to create a sense of satisfaction that comes with completion. It is the ending or **resolution.** (Sometimes a French term, denouement, is used.) It is here that the loose ends are tied up. This tidying up gives the audience a chance to digest the emotions of the crisis and climax. They can see how the character behaved after this upheaval. And it is the playwright's opportunity to make his or her point of view about the events quite clear. When Peter's mother tucks him in bed with camomile tea, we see Peter feeling he'd better think twice before disobeying Mother's warnings. When Maria asks people from each of the warring gangs to carry off Tony's body, we know the author is saying that Maria's love may have helped these people to see beyond their anger toward each other and begin to accept each other's differences. The resolution or ending is very important to your total statement. The lines and the actions are inter-

42

preted perhaps more carefully here than anywhere else in the play. If Maria had told the members of the gangs to leave Tony's body and never to come near her again, we would be left with feelings of deep bitterness and the sense that this struggle would continue indefinitely. If Peter mischievously sneaked out of bed heading for the window once Mother had left the tea for him, we would know we had an incurable adventurer on our hands. The final words and actions carry a lot of weight. Be sure that you've selected them to reflect what you really want to say and that the tone with which you say them contributes to the statement you want to make with your play.

$°°°7°°°$

Language and Action

You may have a play on stage with no words, and you may have a play on radio with no action. In both situations, however, the missing element is implied, because language and action are essential to drama. In a silent play, as you watch a character go through action that makes his or her intentions and feelings clear, you can imagine the thoughts that would be going on in this character's head. When he or she is surprised or angry or delighted, you know what words would come out if they were to be spoken. In a good radio play, when you hear the characters talking together, you know what they are doing. Their lines make clear what they want and how they're going about getting it. Action is not necessarily physical activity, remember; it is what characters do to accomplish what they want.

Action

A play won't work without action. I personally feel action is the more basic of the two ingredients. It is carried out by the characters (people or animals or things) to fulfill their desires. You don't have a drama or a play unless those characters do something to get what they want. That is the action of the piece. It is the same with a game of basketball. The players can be in place with the ball ready, and you know they want to throw the ball through the basket as many times as possible and to keep the opposite team from doing the same, but you have no game until the players begin to play.

Play and Art

It's no accident that the word play is used for both games and drama. It's a word that implies action, movement with an intention or an objective. It also describes a structured situation in life that people created because it's fun and interesting. You don't have to play games or play dramas in order to go on living, but both activities make living a lot more fun and meaningful. Eating, sleeping, working don't seem to be enough to make our lives seem full, not even when you add falling in love and out of love, having and raising children, caring for others, and worshipping a divine force according to your spiritual belief. People need to have play in their lives. (It's interesting to note that higher forms of animals do as well.) It puts their relationships with other people and their awareness of life into another perspective.

People also have a strong need to create works of art. With art we put some of the elements we have in our world into a form that pleases us and reflects our feelings about life. A dramatic play is both an art form, because it rearranges elements of life in order to say something about life,

45

and a game form, because it calls for players to play an action or to act according to certain rules. You know how rules are used for games. In the case of plays, the rules are the form into which we fit the characters and the things they do. The traditional form or rules we use to shape plays has been a part of our culture for hundreds of years. It would be difficult to say whether the ideas you want to express about life "work" more effectively in this form because of the way people naturally see events in life or whether we see them this way because we are so used to this form. Playwrights do try new forms for plays other than using a beginning, middle, and end built around events involving a main character. Sometimes the audience is excited by the new ways. More often new forms for plays make an audience feel upset, and they call the work nonsense or pointless. It takes a while to get used to new forms for things in our lives.

Language

There is form to the way we use language. The rules of grammar govern the way we put words together so they will make sense in our language. We have different categories of words, such as nouns, verbs, adjectives, adverbs, articles. These categories determine how the word is to be used—a noun names something or someone, an adjective describes that thing or person, a verb gives the action or state of being, and so forth. And grammar sets up the rules for how to combine categories of words in sentences so we can use them to communicate information.

Even though you have to stick to the important grammatical rules if you want to be understood, there are many different ways to choose and arrange your words. Your choice represents your style of using your language. It is another kind of form. Because people are complicated beings they developed languages in ways that would communicate complicated thoughts. Within any one language, there are many ways of expressing the same thought. The words chosen not only tell the listener something about the thought but also tell something about the person speaking. The words the speaker chooses give us many levels of information. Consider the following sentences as ways a person could say she feels cold.

"I am chilled to the bone with raw dampness."

"If he don't give us more heat in this dump, I'll give him a present that'll warm him up!"

"That ride just made me a freeze-dried specimen for future generations."

"I'm exhilarated when my skin is red and cold from swimming!"

The statements reflect different kinds of cold, different emotional reactions to the cold, and different kinds of people involved. We are so used to interpreting the style of people's speech that we don't usually stop to analyze it.

Dialogue

As you write plays, it is great fun to make yourself even more aware of the way people speak because your writing then can reflect more of what you hear. The dialogue in a play, the words the characters say, depends on the action in which they are engaged. From what they are saying and the way in which they say it, the actor is led to understand what the character wants. It gives him or her ideas on how to play the action of going about getting it. This process makes the play come alive for the audience. The dialogue also tells the actors what kind of person the character is and will spur him or her on to find the right voice and body movements to use in portraying the role. It would be dull to have all the characters talk in the language you use personally. Try to make each character a separate kind of person with specific attitudes, manners, and social class, and let this be reflected in the person's speech. Analyzing speech is a rather dry way of approaching it. Instead, listen carefully to people around you and see if you can catch what is unique about the way they talk. Sometimes it is the words they like to use. Often it is the rhythm of their sentences. Do they tend to use long, descriptive sentences? Short, fragmented phrases? Self-interruptions and repeats? Pompous statements? Strong starts that trail off without conclusions? As a writer of dialogue, you do not have to be correct in your use of English. You are only reflecting what someone else is saying; it is they who are correct or incorrect. Have fun with this freedom!

The language in your play as a whole needs to have consistency of style, however, even though the individual characters may speak differently from each other. It is hard to describe how to achieve consistency because so much of it depends upon your ear as an artist. In this sense, the words of the whole play are like a piece of music—they create sounds, rhythms, tones that are heard and physically felt. They also create images. In this way dialogue is also poetry, whether or not it rhymes or has a definite meter.

48

Read the dialogue out loud to yourself as you would like it to sound. Does it create the effect you are after? You may want a very pleasing flow from the words. You may want a strong, percussive sound. You may want to reflect the refined language used in a classical myth that you're dramatizing. You may want the flavor of regional speech for a folktale you're dramatizing. Whatever the predominant quality of the dialogue in your play, you'll want to include some variations within the style you've chosen or it will become monotonous and lose its effect. If you find that lines are choppy when you wanted them smooth, or repetitive when you wanted a sharp contrast, make the appropriate changes.

After your own reading aloud, it helps to listen carefully when actors are reading the script—not at a **cold reading** where they will probably stumble over lines, but after they are familiar with it. This is a good time to notice awkward words or phrases. You will hear the rhythm of your lines. They can create laughter or a touching moment. Sometimes you will be immensely pleased! Sometimes you will be shocked because you'd intended an effect opposite from what you got. Let your ear be the guide for making the appropriate adjustments. If you sense something is not quite right but can not identify why, perhaps another sympathetic listener can offer suggestions.

Using Improvisation for Creating Dialogue

You may understand and appreciate differences in the use of language but feel unsure of yourself in actually writing dialogue for the characters. It is often hard to get started with it. If you are having this trouble, it can be helpful to let the actors provide the words as they improvise. Be specific about the various scenes you want them to act out. Make sure everyone is clear about where each scene takes place, what characters are in it, and what the characters want in that situation before the actors start improvising. Even though the actors are making up the words, you will still be the playwright if you are the one setting up the situations and the one in charge of keeping the play developing in the direction you envision. By all means, be open to the ideas and suggestions of the actors as you work together, but if you want this to be your play, let them know in a friendly way at the start that you're the playwright on this particular project.

As the actors improvise, watch and listen carefully. You might find this trial run gives you enough ideas to go home and write on your own. Or you may find you'll want to give the actors suggestions and have them try it again. You may be the kind of person who is better at creating the whole play through improvisation while you all work together. Some plays are developed entirely during the rehearsal process in this way and are never written down, or are written down only after the performance. The words spoken might be different each time the play is rehearsed and performed. However, if the structure of the piece remains the same and the important actions are played each time, it might not matter to you that the dialogue varies. In fact it can be an advantage if your actors are inexperienced because it keeps them fresh and involved and avoids an artificial sound.

50

Using Scenarios

If you choose to work with improvisation rather than giving
the actors exact lines to learn, it is a good idea to write out
scenarios for each of the scenes. A scenario is a brief description of a **scene,** telling its location, the characters involved in it, and the important events that occur during
that scene. The scenario can be given to the actors for each
scene in the play so that they have some notes to refresh
them as they work on their parts between rehearsals. You
can also post the scenarios backstage for the actors to check
before going onstage to improvise their parts. This is how it
was done in the old days of Commedia dell'Arte, a style of
comic plays done originally in Italy during the 1600s and
1700s in which professional actors would perform as the
same set of characters in many different silly situations.
The lines were never written down, but the scenarios were
worked out and tacked up as reminders. It was the player's
job to create funny dialogue and physical **business** to do
with the action.

Writing from Improvised Scenes

It might be important to you to **set** the dialogue rather than
let it be improvised. Perhaps you find the actors change
lines and even actions too much to suit your goals. Maybe
you want a tightly edited version of the play with language
that is precise. Then, by all means, write a script. If you
especially like some of the things the actors have been saying, they probably can help a lot by writing down their own

lines for you to work with. If rehearsals have been producing different dialogue for the scenes each time you do them, try using a tape recorder when you rehearse. Although it takes quite a bit of time to listen to all rehearsals on tape, it will give you several versions to pick from and choose the best dialogue. Another way to use tapes is to listen to the several versions and then, having a sense of the possibilities, write freely from your own memory and impressions. It can happen that the actors never come up with dialogue that sounds right to your ear for the rhythm of the play. Although you may not use any of their words in your final script, their development of the characters and the action still may be very useful to you in imagining exactly how you want that scene to go. Then it is time to go off by yourself and write it out so they will have your words to work with. It always helps to have a picture in your mind of what is happening as you write; improvisations can often give you that picture.

8

Developing Ideas through Improvisation

A good flow of ideas is a blessing. But don't sit around waiting for ideas to appear. Practice in thinking up ideas is one of the best ways to stimulate more. Don't be stingy, fearing that you'll use them up! I was once inspired by an interview with a very creative man in the sciences, Linus Pauling, who was asked how he got so many good ideas. He simply replied that he just thought of lots of them and threw out the ones that weren't any good.

Whether the play you're working on is coming from your own story, from one you've heard, or from a tale in a book, you can enrich it by developing more ideas through improvisation. You might find a more interesting way to do something, a solution for a scene that hasn't been working, or an idea for a new play. Your actors might find ways to create fuller characters. Improvisation will also help a group feel more comfortable as they experiment, test, and share ideas with one another. It helps you move beyond the point of worrying about making mistakes or looking stupid;

you will find it easier to come up with all kinds of interesting material.

Story-building is one way of coming up with lots of plot lines—events that happen to characters. Sit in a circle; have one person begin making up a story by introducing a character or a place or an event. Let each person take a turn at picking up the tale and adding something to it. You can have the person talking decide when to pass it to the next storyteller, or a leader can call "Next" at unexpected times, or you can use a set time limit. It's most fun if the amount of time each person has is short so that everyone is led to think quickly and respond spontaneously, and everyone has more than one turn. Allow people in the circle to pass, however, if they feel stumped when it's their turn, so the story doesn't get bogged down. As you gain skill with this technique, see if you aren't able even to finish one another's sentences without breaking the rhythm of the telling.

Story-building could be centered around a picture or photograph that everyone has studied, or each person in your group could have a different picture and some time alone to create a story from it that they tell to the group. Another variation is to look for interesting people around you whom you don't know and make up a story about one of them. Working from pictures or real people can be used by anyone working alone, too. Write down your ideas or speak into a tape recorder and collect thoughts to write in a journal and perhaps share with others later.

Opening lines are fun for jogging your imagination. Have everyone make up a provocative sentence for someone else to use as the start of a story or the start of a scene that a group could act out with improvisation. Notice the different situations that come to mind when different details are mentioned:

"If you don't move by the time I count three, you're going to get it!"

"Get out of that bed now or the movers will pack you into the van with it!"

"Good morning, Mira, are you ready for the big day?"

"Bob, help me put tape around the windows to keep the sand from blowing in."

Work quickly, whether you're story-building in a circle or having groups act out a scene. The pressure of time usually helps you find ideas without killing too many with criticism. When you're acting out scenes, give the group only a few minutes to decide *who* is involved, *where* they are, and *what* they are doing. The actors should create it as they improvise rather than making it up in advance. Wonderful ideas come to us spontaneously when we're involved in action. Just remind the actors and yourself that you need to find out what your character wants and what she or he does to get it. Find the solution while acting with the rest of the team playing in the scene.

Making up *closing lines* is another way to go. Use them as you did opening lines but starting, of course, from the other end of the story:

"It seems impossible now, but I know we'll come back some day."

"If we keep our pact, no one ever needs to know."

"Now, tell me the truth. Did you ever once suspect it was me?"

When you hear the line that ends the story or the play,

let a flood of impressions flow out—sounds, pictures of scenes, images of characters and objects. If you're working in a group, be sure everyone is able to share the thoughts quickly before people accept or reject them. From the collection, decide which ones to enact. Or, if you're writing, jot down the ideas and fragments of ideas before eliminating any or putting them into complete story form.

Telegrams are a variation on the closing lines. Make the events of the scene lead up to a character sending a telegram, such as:

ATTACKED AND ROBBED. SEND I.D. AND MONEY IN CARE OF EMBASSY. BERT

BASEMENT FLOODED. FURNACE BROKEN. CHILDREN HAVE MEASLES. PLEASE RETURN. MONA

FOUND HELPFUL GUIDE AND GREAT SITE FOR DIGGING. EXTENDING STAY. MCCARTHY

When using a line or telegram as the ending of the scene or short play, in addition to being open to the flood of images it evokes, try asking yourself what question the play had set out to answer. In the last one, for instance, if the question were whether or not Susan McCarthy would learn to strike out on her own as a mining surveyor you would have a very different play than if the question concerned whether or not shy Jack McCarthy, who'd chosen a vacation of joining an archaeological dig in order to meet people, would find a girl friend.

WHO, WHERE, and WHAT draw bags will let you stretch by putting unlikely or unexpected elements together in a way that makes sense. Have everyone think of several interesting places for the **setting** of a play. Use a separate piece of paper for writing down each one and drop them all

56

into a bag marked WHERE. Then think of interesting characters and write down a description for the WHO bag. The WHO's could be very brief clues like "detective" or "ten-year-old student" or descriptions that include age, personality, likes and dislikes, profession or occupation. It helps if the sex of the person can be left undetermined, unless you want to have separate bags for girls and boys or like to give people practice playing roles of the opposite sex. For the WHAT bag, cook up a variety of things people could be doing and put these on slips of paper to drop inside. Keep the WHAT suggestions short and specific, allowing the reasons for someone doing that activity to come out of the playing. Examples of WHAT's might be "playing cards," "wrapping packages for mailing," "putting on costumes."

When your draw bags are ready, have the actors each draw a WHO for themselves. The group they are in then draws a WHERE and a WHAT to use together. Let them start playing with as little planning as possible. As players become more experienced, they'll be able to make clear to themselves and the audience whether or not there are many cars parked in the "city parking garage" in which they find themselves "playing cards." Spontaneous discoveries are often hilarious and always exhilarating. You can use these draw bags as a writing exercise as well. Three slips of paper can get you going with some unexpected elements to turn into a story or a play.

Playing with *objectives and actions* is yet another way of using a technique that helps both actors and writers. Remember that the objective is what the character wants in a given situation and the action is what he or she does to get it. An example of an objective, or the thing a character wants, could be "to get people to notice me." An action she might play to be noticed could be "being helpful." She might also try "being obnoxious," which would be a totally different way of going about getting noticed. Suppose what the character wanted was "to find out a piece of information." An action to get it could be "asking questions." A more indirect approach could be "flattering a person into talking." Thinking of motivations and strategies for characters in this way can be a lot of fun. You can work with it by first deciding on the WHO, WHERE, and WHAT of a situation before adding the objective and action, or you could start with the action alone and in the playing or writing let it become clear to you what the character really wants, who he is, where he is, and what he's doing there.

If you're finding one of the characters not very interesting, try giving him or her a different action, another strategy for getting what he or she wants. Sometimes just a simple change makes all the difference. Suppose the character is a teenager who wants permission from her parents to take an after-school job. You may have had her being sweet and helpful at home to win them over to her reasoning. What happens to the scene if she pulls a stubborn silent act or becomes loud and demanding or outrageous?

You could also try changing what a character wants. In some versions of *Hansel and Gretel* both parents love the children and want to help them find their way home after searching for food. In others, the stepmother wants to get rid of them because there isn't enough food to go around. Suppose you had been working with the former version and found it too bland. Then try giving the stepmother the objective of getting rid of those kids and have her doing it with the action or strategy of being caring. Because her underlying wish has changed, that caring now becomes a piece of trickery rather than an act of love. This change may give you the extra tension your play needs.

Any of these suggestions for setting up and making variations for improvisations can be used as writing suggestions. If you can visualize the ideas right away, then begin writing. If it's difficult to imagine how the action would work, or if you are at a loss to know how to get started writing, it can help a lot to see actors using suggestions in improvisations. Then try writing. Let them act out your version. Make changes in the script or give the actors new situations to improvise. The more familiar you become with seeing the play move back and forth between the written page and the stage, the easier it will be for you to create the play.

∘∘∘9∘∘∘

Three Freezes:
A Useful
Format for Improvised Plays

A freeze in theater is a scene in which the motion is caught in stillness; sometimes it's called a tableau. It's fun to see if a group of you can compose a scene that is absolutely still, like a three-dimensional picture, and will communicate a lot of information about the characters in it. A good way to start practicing is with a simple game called Sculptors and Statues. Instead of spinning your partner around and letting him or her freeze where landing, as you do in the playground game of Statues, have one person mold a partner into a statue of a person or animal doing something. Decide beforehand what the category of activity is to be so that you'll have a whole gallery of statues of people playing a sport or doing a job or practicing an art. When all are ready, see if the other sculptors can guess what the absolutely still statues are doing. Once all have been identified by the viewers and sculptors (remember the statues are frozen and unable to answer any questions), the partners switch roles and the new sculptors make their partners into different statues. It takes a little practice for actors to learn to hold absolutely still, not even moving their eyes, yet keeping alive the emotion and concentration of a character engaged in a certain activity! The sculptors also need practice in finding the most effective positions by which to communicate what they have in mind.

Move on to having sculptors become directors who use several actors and make a group scene of an activity. The next step would be to have the scene show a highly dramatic moment. To find these moments, pick a theme such as feelings or dreams or holidays. If you're working with feelings, for instance, you could ask each person participating to remember being very scared or very angry. You might remember a specific nightmare or a favorite holiday at its most wonderful moment. Let the director use several players to form the situation he or she has in mind and cast one of the actors to play himself or herself in the scene. If you have enough people, more than one director can work at a time, and the teams take turns becoming audience for each other when you perform.

When you're ready to show the tableau, let the director ask the audience to turn their backs or close their eyes until the actors have responded to a count of "One, two, three, freeze." Once the tableau is in place, the audience looks. Can they determine what is happening in the frozen scene? Whose story is it—in other words, who is the protagonist? Who are the other characters? The more careful the director is in placing the characters in the space, the more immediately the scene will communicate the meaning of the moment. It also helps if actors are fully involved in capturing the way their characters feel at that instant. As you gain practice in doing these scenes, you will amaze yourself with the amount of information you are able to communicate.

To turn the tableaus into plays, start with the most intense moment of memory: the peak of the surprise, the most terrifying moment in the nightmare, the most wonderful moment of that holiday celebration. Think of this tableau as the middle of your play, or the crisis moment. Know that everything you'll include prior to this moment will lead up to it; it is the high point of tension when the main character must do something to determine the outcome. Think of a good place to begin your story that will lead you to this point of crisis. You may want to begin only a few minutes before the crisis, or perhaps a few weeks before. Don't make it so early in time that you'll lose the connection or so close to the crisis that there's no opportunity to build tension. Sometimes it's hard to use a situation that happened to you because you become more concerned with making it accurate than with picking a good beginning moment that will put the play into motion. Also, the actual way the incident began may be too upsetting to you to want to work with it, or may not be very dramatic. Try using only the moment of crisis and ask others to help make up beginning and ending moments. The ending moment, of course, shows what happened as a result of the surprise or how the scary dream turned out or the happy holiday came to a close. Let it be the very last thing that happens in your play.

Present the three freezes in sequence: beginning, middle, and end. Have the actors move into place as the director calls, "One, two, three, freeze." It's good to establish a steady, slow rhythm for doing this such as:

"Ready? Move, two, three; freeze." (Continue holding on silent beats of two, three; one, two, three.)

"And, move, two, three; freeze" (two, three; one, two, three).

"And, move, two, three; freeze" (two, three; one, two, three).

"And, break."

It's like counting music with the "ready" and the "and" as an upbeat to help the players start together on the "move," which is the down beat on the count one. Being this formal helps you and the audience see the content of the picture without being distracted by messy edges of sound or movement.

When you and the audience have looked at the sequence a few times, you'll know if you've found the right three moments to tell the whole story. If not, make changes in the way you set them up. Perhaps you'll realize that one of the actual moments chosen wasn't the strongest one for capturing the tale. Find a more effective one. The questions you asked when evaluating drafts of improvisations or written scripts are appropriate here. Whose story is it? Do all three moments directly concern this person? Do all three moments directly relate to the main issue? Examples of main issues are: the time I was scared by my friends in the middle of the night of my birthday; the nightmare I had of the ground opening up and swallowing me; the Thanksgiving feast my family held in the woods at my aunt's camp. Tell the story through action instead of talk, since no words are involved at this point. Are the actions that the characters are catching in the freeze the most telling ones? Are all the characters involved and contributing to the situation?

Does the style of the three moments feel related? Realistic? Fantastic? Intense, but low-key?

When the three tableaus of your stories are as you want them, it's time for the actors to practice improvising all the action and talk that occurs between each of those moments. Start them with "Ready? One, two, three; freeze, and play the scene." The first few times through, have the actors freeze when they reach the middle moment to assure that everyone is aware of it and can move into it at the same time. After a pause they continue playing until the ending moment, when everyone freezes. No more action or dialogue may occur after this freeze. The actors are released from it with "And, break."

Critique the play as you have done with other improvisations. You'll find that a common tendency is for people to rush from one freeze to the next, causing the whole play to last only a minute or two. As your group notes the parts that work well and strengthens the sections that are weak, they'll find lots more interesting action and business to play leading up to the crisis and through the climax to the end. Encourage this fuller playing because it usually produces good material. It is always easy to trim things back if you want a tighter, shorter piece for your final product. Once the group is well in tune, it is no longer necessary for them to freeze at the middle moment; the actors will be able to sense its approach and pass through it together without stopping the action. But using a middle freeze in early rehearsals gives them a structure that helps hold the piece together and gives the improvisation sharpness. The audience does not have to be aware of how it is achieved, although sometimes it's fun for them to see the three freezes first as a preview so that they'll appreciate seeing the way your players work as a team between the three freezes.

Using this approach of identifying a crisis moment and then creating an effective beginning and closing moment can be useful in turning a variety of material into plays. Although it's a particularly helpful technique for giving structure to personal stories, it also works well for dramatizing history or a current news story. The three moments give dramatic form to human events that we don't ordinarily think of in terms of play form. You can try it with stories to see if this structure is more helpful to you than outlining events as suggested in Chapter Three. You can try it with purely imagined events, too, to make a fantasy piece. Always be sure to include strong human feelings in the crisis moment. Without involving these feelings, it will be difficult to identify a good beginning and ending that will make an exciting play.

A play does not have to be written in script form to be considered finished. Scripting it is the tightest way to preserve it for others to read or perform in the future. However, you could record the structure you used without the dialogue. You could describe the exact moments you created as three freezes with the feelings and issues involved in them. Then actors and directors in the future can work with the material in their own fashion, given more leeway than they'd have with a script. Whether performing artists work from structures and ideas or from scripts, the performances that come from one production will be unlike performances from another production of the same play. Remember, a script is like a recipe: If your cooks are artists, no two soups come out exactly the same.

ооо 10 ооо

Writing a Play
from Your Own Ideas

Much of the focus in this book has been on thinking of
things that happen to people in story form and then picking
out elements of those stories to arrange in a form that will
make them work as a play. As you've read through the
previous chapters and thought about the ideas or tried
some of the suggestions, you may very well have come up
with ideas of your own for writing a play that aren't tied to
a story at all. Or you may have had a strong idea for a play
all along and have been looking for a way to get started
on it.

Now that you're somewhat familiar with the elements
needed in a play (characters, actions, locations) and the
structure of a play (opening situation, beginning action, development, crisis, climax, and ending) you probably are beginning to see that you can work with many different
sources of ideas and use them as the basis of a play. I hope
you also realize by now that there is not one correct route
to follow. What stimulates one person will not turn on another; what is effective for you on one project may not

work on the next. With creative work we must be flexible and open to new ways of doing things while still being aware of guidelines and "rules" that help keep us on track. Use any of the suggestions in previous chapters to help shape your ideas. Some of them are referred to here again from a slightly different perspective; some new approaches are also given for you to consider.

Personal Incident

An incident from *your life* may be a good source for an original play. It could be about a time of very strong feeling, such as being scared to death or being furious. It could be about a time you were faced with a very difficult challenge with which you struggled and which you succeeded in meeting. It could be about a funny episode in which you expected things to go a certain way and everything went wrong but you had fun anyway. Then there're *dreams*; perhaps you've had a dream that was unusual and eerie and you'd like to shape it into a play.

To get started, you could try the format of three freezes discussed in Chapter Nine and identify the most intense moment of crisis. Then think back to select a good beginning and ahead to pick an effective ending. Or you could work with your idea in the terms discussed in Chapter Six: The Form of a Play. Identify the main character or protagonist. It might very well be you, if it's your dream or your life incident. But you also might feel the play would work better if someone else were the main character. Then decide who is the secondary character, the person the main character is very involved with in some way. What does the main character want to do? Who gets in his or her way? This person would be the antagonist or third character. When you're clear about these principal characters, you can fill in the other, minor ones around them as you select the key events. What will the opening situation be? Next decide on the best beginning action that will upset the situation. From there, events unfold. Carefully select the number of scenes and their physical location so that the play is tight and not rambling. Develop the action up to the point of crisis when the main character is faced with an important decision. This decision will cause the events to go one way or the other and answer the key question of your piece. Once this character makes the choice, you'll have the high emotional point of the play in the climax, where we see the result of his or her decision. And write a brief ending in which we see the situation resolved. If this summary sounds confusing to you as you read it here, go back to Chapter Six for the fuller explanation. If it's hard to imagine how certain scenes would work, try writing a draft and have actors do a **reading** for you so you can hear the lines spoken. If you're having trouble thinking of the actual dialogue for the characters to speak, ask the actors to try improvising the scene you describe before you write your first draft. If this still seems confusing, try to think of your incident or dream as a story and go back to the ideas discussed in Chapters Three and Four where the elements of a play are pulled from story form in a simpler manner.

Character

Working from character is another way to develop your own play. Try starting with *two-character scenes;* they're fun to do and often easier to shape than scenes with lots of people. If you alone or you and your friends write several scenes, you could present them together as a unit instead of one longer play. If you're working with actors, get two to work as a team and have each decide on a character to portray. If you're working alone, you decide on two characters to create. The characters could be people, animals, or objects.

Introduce the characters to the audience by making clear what they routinely do. Keep this fairly simple by establishing one activity, such as a soda can that has to wait for people to buy it, drink from it, and then recycle it, or a newspaper that gets read and thrown down or thrown away.

Next have each character let the audience (and possibly the other character) know what his or her strongest wish or very secret desire is. Perhaps the soda can wishes it could lead a more permanent existence and be saved by someone and made into a lamp, and the newspaper is tired of making people unhappy when they read awful news printed on it and wants to be made into paper airplanes, party hats, and other fun toys.

Now decide if you want the characters to help each other reach their secret goal or hinder each other in reaching the goal. The newspaper might feel sympathetic because it also has a temporary kind of life; therefore, it offers to help the soda can rig itself up as a lamp, and the can then helps the newspaper fold itself into an origami shape by rolling over its folds. Or each could be jealous of the other's intent to attract a person's interest, and they compete with each other.

69

You could find an ending for the scene at this point or continue by introducing a new problem for one of the characters, such as the can getting dented in its attempt to jump onto a table, or a problem for both of them, such as some toddlers who enter and begin messing things up. By the way, you can continue with just two actors by having them respond to the toddlers as though they were there without actually having other actors portray them. The audience will "see" them if the can and the newspaper react to them fully. A problem, of course, represents new possibilities for the characters. It could be set up as a promise that turns into a problem and brings about a crisis, such as a person entering whom they both hope will use them, but who instead steps on them, denting and ripping them. Or it could seem to be a problem, such as the arrival of the toddlers, that then turns into a solution, such as having the children turn both the can and newspaper into toys—the can as part of a tower, perhaps, and the newspaper a roof for a house.

However you decide to do it, be sure to have the characters reach a crisis in which things become tense, and then do something to get out of it. Conclude with a resolution so we'll feel the question of the little play has been answered: Were the characters' wishes fulfilled?

You can use the same approach with human characters, such as a window washer who wants to become an airplane pilot and a plumber who wants to become a singing star. Two people might want to use the same object or place for two very different things, such as a man clearing an empty lot of trash in order to park his new car there and a kid clearing it to practice ball there. Once you start making up such characters who have clear but simple desires, your mind will surprise you by coming up with more and more!

Writing a Play from Your Own Ideas

Creating a *principal character* is the way many playwrights begin. Imagine this character very fully. You might use someone you know as a source of inspiration or just create the character completely from your imagination. Fill in many details about the person's past and what he or she wants, what problems face him or her, how he or she behaves with other people. As you create this person's life, you'll get ideas about whom to create as the important secondary character, the person with whom the main character is closely involved. And you'll form an idea about who is opposing this main character in getting what he or she wants; this will be the antagonist in your play. Find the important events in your main character's life that you think will make an interesting play about him or her. Use the same suggestions given for working with an incident from your life: Identify the beginning moment, the crisis, climax, and ending. When you are very clear about who this character is and what is important to him or her, it won't be hard to find answers for these other questions.

Situation

For some people it's easier and more fun to start with situations that are interesting and exciting rather than with characters. You might like to cook up a good plot line for a mystery or imagine an event like a circus, a car accident, tryouts for a team or a play, a social party with dancing, getting lost in the woods, being kidnapped. Fill in the details as you imagine the situation. Try telling a good friend about it; the ideas can flow more easily when you're trying to amuse someone you like.

As the events unfold, become clearer about what characters are involved, what they want, what they're doing to get it. Or you may first see what they are doing in the situation and then figure out what **motivation** is underlying their actions. Be careful to avoid having characters doing something for no reason. Their activities need to be related to what they want in the situation.

Also be sure that the things the characters are doing and the way they are interacting with each other says something about life that you want to share with the audience. Of course you want your play to be enjoyable—perhaps scary, funny, or moving. And you want people in the audience to be interested in it and to laugh and perhaps to feel like crying. But you also want them to sense that it all leads up to something. If they say, "What's the point?" when it's over, you haven't thought your play through enough.

Theme

Sometimes it seems appropriate to start your play by thinking about the message you want to give the audience. The message is often closely tied to the theme. For instance, you may want to write a play about friendship. This would be its theme. The message would be what you want to say about friendship. Perhaps you'd like to explore what happens to friends when jealousies arise or the difficulties of building new friendships in a school where there are strong cliques. Some themes deal with personal issues such as feelings, boyfriends or girl friends, lying, loving, getting on with people in our families. Some deal with issues in the world around us like drugs, or student rights, or immigrating to a new country, or politics.

72

Writing a Play from Your Own Ideas

You may want to approach your play first through its theme and message because an issue is strong in your mind and you want to try to sort it out for yourself and share it with others. You may want to create a play to use for a particular occasion on which a given theme is called for, such as Brotherhood Week or the Fourth of July. Remember that you will be communicating your ideas through a play. Don't try to lecture or give arguments in a play as you would in a speech. A play presents its ideas indirectly through characters living through a situation. It is their action and interaction with others that shows us a reflection of our lives.

As you think about your theme, you'll want to let images of people and events and places and action come to mind. Imagine characters doing things. Try to get in touch with the feelings *they* might have—not just your own feelings—as several different attitudes and points of view will be represented by the various characters. See the characters wrangling and tangling with each other, liking each other, opposing each other, helping each other. Keep a record of the many situations, scenes, characters that occur to you and begin to select those that feel appropriate to the theme and that seem as though they could make a good play. Then begin to work with one and shape it as we've discussed before, identifying the principal character and the beginning, middle, and end of the events that happen to him or her.

ooo 11 ooo

When You Don't Have Time to Do a Whole Play

You may find yourself in a situation where you'd like to give a presentation, but you don't have skilled actors or people interested in devoting enough time to rehearse a finished play. Or perhaps you suddenly realize you need something to present for a particular occasion and there aren't enough days left to rehearse a full play. Plays are complicated events and take a lot of time to prepare, as you no doubt realize! By simplifying some of the elements used, however, you can often make a very interesting presentation that may be easier than a play. If you think about plays as using the elements of characters, action, and dialogue, and if you recall that the events are shaped into a sequence having a beginning, middle, and end, it might help you see how and where you could simplify by eliminating one or more elements.

You could use a series of tableaus showing characters in dramatic situations. Let these "pictures" illustrate the theme of your exhibit. Say your goal is to commemorate Martin Luther King's birthday. In a large space like the school cafeteria, gym, library, or a community room in your neighborhood, several groups of people could form scenes from his life or scenes showing conditions of segregation during the 1960s in this country and various actions that civil rights activists took under Dr. King's leadership to challenge these conditions. It is easier to identify several key moments that are dramatic and representative of this theme than it is to create a whole play about it. If the moments are well chosen and portrayed with real conviction, the total effect can be powerful. The audience could be invited to wander through a gallery of such "pictures" or could be guided slowly along a path you prescribed, assuring they would see them in the sequence you prefer. Because it could be difficult for actors to hold such freezes for more than a few minutes, you could have them alternate between two or three pictures; the moving between tableaus will give them relief. Or you could have a team for each tableau (perhaps one class responsible for each), and the different performers would spell each other. It could be like the changing of the guard at a national monument!

There's no reason why you couldn't use this approach to prepare a live birthday card for someone in your family. Have friends and family create tableaus to show the birthday person's life or to show wonderful things you're going to do for him or her during the coming year as an extended present! The players could form all the tableaus in the same spot or set them up in several rooms so the birthday person discovers them in different places.

Try using a narrator to tell a story while the actors perform the action without dialogue as the story is told. Some rehearsal will be needed, of course, to develop interesting action and to coordinate the narrator and the actors, but the actors will not have to memorize lines or the sequence of action because they will be cued by the words of the story being told by the narrator. The storyteller could actually use a book to prompt him or her. You could present this very simply with no sets or costumes if you were to visit a small audience in a classroom, library, or nursing home. Or you could make it an elaborate production involving sets, costumes, masks, or make-up, music, and so forth, and present it in a formal space like an auditorium, outdoor plaza, or playground. By the way, this is a useful approach if you need to perform in a large space where it would be difficult for the actors' voices to be heard; the narrator could have a microphone while the others communicate through their movement. You might even have a whole group of actors at microphones to one side of the stage, each one paired with a "moving" actor so that the voice and action of each character is done by a team. This variation is more complicated than using just one speaker, however, and would need more rehearsal.

Use a series of short scenes that have developed from improvisation or short stories. Suppose none of them is a complete play and they do not lend themselves to being worked into a unified play; present them as what they really are: several short scenes. They might be creative work that has come out of a class, or work that individuals have done on their own for fun, or scenes that different groups have worked out on a common theme. If you know in advance that you'd like to use this format, you could all agree on a particular theme (families, dreams, a day in my life, peace as I'd like to see it) and have different groups or individuals create a scene dealing with this subject. In selecting the ones to include, try to balance the styles used. If some have full action and dialogue and some are silent or silently acted with a single narrator speaking, present them in an order that will help the audience adjust to the different styles. It's often effective to present them with a connecting device, such as using a Master of Ceremonies who introduces them; showing slides of a similar theme; playing music; having other performers sing, dance, or perform little acts like telling jokes or a running gag. An example of a running gag could be a character who comes out at each interlude to do something like play a cello or give instructions, but each time he appears, someone or something interrupts: a street sweeper, an elephant, a street band, cops chasing someone, etc. It's fun to think of interesting interludes, but obviously you'll want to pick the kind of connecting device that sets the right mood for the presentation of your scenes and contributes to the whole event.

You and your group may have created several scenes for a play but find you do not have time to finish working them into a completed whole before you must disband or before the special date has arrived when you wanted to present. You might consider using a narrator to provide the necessary connections as though he or she were telling you a story with several illustrations—in other words, the scenes that are ready. Or it might be effective to have one of the characters in the play tell the story to the audience about the main character; he or she could step in and out of the scenes that come to life. The main character could be the one who tells the story and who steps back and forth between speaking directly to the audience and moving into the scene that's ready to be enacted.

Improvised scenes are another alternative to a full play. If your group has spent time together with acting exercises and improvising, present this work. Don't try to show techniques you haven't practiced because your lack of skill will be evident and you won't hold the audience's attention. But often you've gotten quite a bit of experience with techniques that might not seem worth showing but that could actually be very interesting to an audience if they understand what you're working on. For instance, suppose you were to do WHO, WHERE, and WHAT draw bags. The scenes you create from this format can be as much fun for the audience as for the actors if they too know the conditions. There's no advance planning and the audience is told the three elements at the same time the actors are given them. Perhaps the audience could be invited to add suggestions to the draw bags. If your actors are not yet able to handle three new elements from the draw bags, have them do one at a time. True, it's a simple acting exercise, but it can be very amusing for the audience to see how the situation changes when you alter only one of the three elements, keeping the other two as your real situation. For instance, the actors continue to be themselves, setting up the stage and welcoming the audience, but they do it as though everyone were at the bottom of an empty swimming pool. Or the actors set up the stage and welcome the audience in the room you're actually using, but they behave as trained dogs or some other characters quite different from themselves. Try scenes based on the opening lines or closing lines or telegrams. Do two-character scenes. Show several sets of three freezes. If you've rehearsed the action in between the tableaus, play these stories out completely.

There are many other ideas for improvisation in the books recommended on pages 103-06. Use structures that you've had fun and success with. Always have a clear structure, because improvising scenes or plays without structure will just give you chaos. And presenting improvisation using structures you have not practiced with will just give you unpredictable work.

And, of course, if you have been writing a play but don't have time to rehearse and produce it, a solution is to present a **reading** of your script. Use different actors for each character and have someone—perhaps you—read the stage directions. Practice it several times to get beyond the stumbling of a cold reading and everyone can read with expression. Have the actors sit or stand in a good light where everyone can be seen and heard. If you have extra time, you could take it a step further with a staged reading. Here the actors would be given **blocking** and play the parts with action while still holding the scripts in hand. If a group of you have been writing plays, a reading of several of these could make a very interesting presentation. It also is a helpful step for you as playwright to get reaction from an audience; this kind of feedback will give you ideas for how to improve your script even further.

∘∘∘ 12 ∘∘∘

Using Rehearsals to Refine Your Script

People who work alone to write scripts may not realize the rehearsal process can be very helpful to them. A playwright with a very clear picture in his or her mind about how the play will work onstage might think it is enough to give the finished script to the director and actors to prepare. The writer who has worked with improvisations before writing might feel the script has already gotten its benefit from the acting process. You'll be surprised every time! Even the most experienced writers need to make changes after seeing actors work with their scripts and audiences react to their plays. Professional writers look for opportunities to see their scripts in rehearsal to discover problems that were hidden. Plays that are produced professionally often go through one or more workshop productions where the playwright can work with the director and actors during rehearsal, all of them giving and listening to suggestions, and observe the audiences' reactions during performances. These performances may be attended by outside evaluators who have been asked to share their reactions. Even when a new script is considered ready for full production, the writer is present during the rehearsal, often rewriting scenes from one rehearsal to the next or from one preview performance to the next. In these professional situations, the people involved want the play to become the best it possibly can be, not only for artistic reasons but also because the venture has become a business investment, and they know that if audiences and critics don't really love it, it won't have a long run of performances.

Let us hope that at this stage, the business considerations of your project have not become an important issue, but pride in your work certainly is always involved. The pleasure of feeling you've reworked your play until it's just the way you want it is a great reward. Nothing is more satisfying than having an idea and shaping it into a form that works, a form that pleases you and communicates to others!

A Checklist for Fine Tuning

The next few pages review some of the points given in Chapters Four and Six and give additional ones that may help you.

1. *Whose story is it?* You've heard this question more than once. Even though the answer may have been clear to you as you wrote and read the script, seeing it interpreted by actors might make you realize that the emphasis may not be as strong as you had thought. If it is because the personality of an actor playing a secondary role is so strong that attention is drawn to him or her instead of the main character, perhaps it is just a matter of having the per-

former tone down his or her portrayal. You might realize, however, that you have given this secondary character more interesting things to do and say than the principal one. Look for action and dialogue that will make the audience more interested in and feel closer to the protagonist. You may have to add another scene, or extend one, or shorten another.

2. *Do you care about the main character?* This is a difficult question to ask yourself. Now that the fictitious character has become a real person through the production, you may feel as if you are criticizing someone personally. But remember it is a play, and you can change things in it. You must ask the question bluntly and answer it honestly, because if your main character doesn't work, the play won't either. Sometimes others watching can help you, if they're people whose opinions you trust. If you discover that people don't really care about the main character, see if you can tell why and then make the changes necessary to correct this. It might not take much adjusting to get the right balance. One doesn't need to like everything about the character. Interesting, believable characters often have traits that are not so nice. In fact you may have made the mistake of creating a goody-goody that no one really feels close to. If the character is too perfect, it shouldn't be too hard to create a flaw. Could it be a short temper? A tendency to exaggerate the truth? Impatience with a younger brother? Maybe you realize we don't know why the character does the things he or she does; you'll then need to find a few more ways to have the character show or tell you what is on his mind. It's important that we know what this person wants and what he is going to do to get it. Maybe the

character is too timid, and you wish she could speak up more often and not let others take over as much. Or perhaps she is too much of a loud mouth and grates on your nerves. The chances are that if you look objectively, you will sense what is wrong and have ideas for fixing it. And, of course, you may look at your piece and feel that the main character is just right as is.

3. *Is the play as a whole interesting?* That's another hard question, since it's your creation. Ask others if it's interesting to them as well. Is it fun to see? If you wanted it to be funny, is it? Did you want it to be moving? Does it touch your heart? Is it clear what the play is about, what the main issue is? Have you told the tale through action rather than by having people stand around talking about it? If you find it's not interesting, one of the ways to find a solution is to ask what you or others would like to see happen or wish had happened. Some people might say they wished the character of the grandmother had not died, for instance. You too may feel that way, but you know that this sorrow over her death is important to the theme of your play. If someone says, however, "It didn't make sense to me to have the grandmother die there," that reaction lets you know that the preceding events didn't lead up to the death in a way to make it believable or feel moving. Don't let the main character have too easy a time getting what he or she wants. Complications for the protagonist help make the play "interesting."

4. *Are the elements of character and action well balanced?* In rehearsal you may realize there are too many characters for the length of the play because there isn't enough time to let us know all of them. You could eliminate some or de-

velop only a few. You may have created some interesting action but realize it takes far too long for the purpose it serves in the play. For instance, if a character is to sneak up on some others in order to overhear their plans, you might have created an elaborate scene in which the character finds a hiding place, is almost discovered, but manages to stay undetected while the other characters describe in detail their plans. Although the scene is exciting, it may not be a very important scene in terms of the whole story. Giving it this much attention will detract from the effect of the whole play; therefore, find a way to abbreviate the action.

A common mistake writers or directors make with plays is putting a long piece of physical activity, such as a group dance or a chase scene, in the middle of a play they fear has become a little dull. They hope the activity will perk up the audience's interest. It will throw the piece out of balance, however, unless there has been dancing or other full movement elsewhere in the piece. It is not that these elements need to be evenly distributed, but they do have to balance each other. A long slow build of tension throughout the play could erupt into a wild chase or fight or hell's-a-popping ending. You can feel whether or not you've created enough tension to balance the outburst, just as you can feel whether or not you've balanced people of uneven weight along a seesaw to get it to work. Look at all the characters and action in this way to check their balance with each other.

5. *Have you been economical?* Look at your use of locations in which the action occurs with this same consideration of balance. How many settings have you used? How many scenes occurred in each? Is more time being spent in

moving the **scenery** than in playing the action? Have you gained enough, for example, from having a scene take place in the mountains to pay for the time it took to shift scenery, characters, and action there?

Be economical in all your choices. You don't want more characters or scenes or events than are necessary to tell the tale. You don't want things lasting longer than necessary to say what needs to be said or to do what needs to be done. Checking the actual length of things will give you an important clue, as will checking how things are distributed throughout the piece from beginning to end. And remember that people's emotional reaction to the feeling of balance is as important as the more mechanical measurements of length. Look at all the parts of the play to weigh the time, space, and interest devoted to any part against the importance of that part to the whole.

6. *Is the dialogue the right amount and in the right style?* When you have the major things like characters, action, and number of scenes balanced, listen to the words of the play. Is the amount of dialogue right for the amount of action? Does it feel thin, like the dialogue from a comic book? Is there so much talking that it seems to go on forever before anyone does anything? An actor once told me of a funny time when he was delivering a very long speech in a play, and a child from the audience called out, "Get on with it or get off the stage!" Save yourself this embarrassment by being sure that you don't have characters standing around talking without revealing anything. The actual length of the speech is only a minor clue as to whether or not the speech is too long or short. What the speech gives the audience is the more important concern. Shakespeare

wrote many long speeches for characters in his plays, but the words he used and the thoughts they expressed were so effective in leading us to understand the characters and to reflect on our own lives that people continue to read, perform, and attend his plays almost four hundred years after they were written! It is hard to write long speeches that are effective, however. Be sure yours are not longer than they should be.

Check all dialogue, short or long, for its content. Does it give us information we need to know? About the situation? About the person speaking? About other characters? Has it given us more than is appropriate? For example, if a character talks at length about how much he'd love to be outdoors in winter, we are led to understand that either this is a very important issue for him or he is using it to impress someone. The audience will expect this to come up again in the play. If you intended his long speech only to show him making pleasant remarks to others who have come in from skiing, however, you'll need to trim the speech to create the right balance.

See if the dialogue is appropriate for the character. Are the words you used the kinds of words those characters would speak? Do they flow in a way that would be natural to that person? Do you have the right rhythm for each character? Rehearsal is very helpful for testing this. Inappropriate dialogue will jump out at you when you hear it spoken. Sometimes you'll find that an actor repeatedly trips over some of the lines. Perhaps together you can find a more natural way for this character to speak.

Listen to the rhythm of all the dialogue as though it were a piece of music. Does it create the overall effect you want?

Do the rhythm and sound of the words work well with those of the scenes before and after it? Are things too similar to the point of being a little boring? Too varied to be consistent? Listening without looking can enable you to hear things that were not noticeable while you watched the action.

You can check the rhythm and timing of the whole piece as you go along as well as in your final rewriting. The words and the action and the shifting of locale and the numbers of characters all make up the rhythm. Although you may not have thought about it consciously before now, you probably already have a very good ear for rhythm from seeing plays and movies and television and from listening to music. You are able to feel when a speech or some action drags or builds, when it is monotonous or exciting or when it moves too fast. Now, as the creator instead of the audience, it is your turn to make the adjustments that will get the play just the way you want it.

∘∘∘ 13 ∘∘∘

The Written Form for a Script

There are a few methods of putting your script onto a page that are generally accepted. Their purpose is to make it easier for the actor to read his or her part and know what to do or for the reader to visualize what the play would look like in action.

Clear handwriting or typing is a big help. When a person is trying to read her character's lines with good expression and feeling, she doesn't want to have to struggle with interpreting handwriting. Typing is the easiest to read but not always possible to do. Good printing is almost as legible. If your own printing is not clear, see if you can swap favors with someone who could do a good job of copying for you.

Consistent margins are a big help as your eye scans the page. There is more than one style used, however. One style places the character's name in the center of the page with the line that person speaks below the name. Other styles place the character's names on the left side of the page. The lines of dialogue should use consistent margins on the right and left or share the left margin with the character's name. See the illustration below. Notice that the character's name is always written in capital letters to distinguish it clearly from the dialogue.

> #### WILBER
> I don't understand why you don't believe me when I tell you I'm her half-brother. We grew up in the same family.
>
> #### JEANNE
> But you don't look anything alike! You even talk with different accents.
>
> #### WILBER
> (Laughing) We fool around a lot.

*   *   *

WILBER: I don't understand why you don't believe me when I tell you I'm her half-brother. We grew up in the same family.

JEANNE: But you don't look anything alike! You even talk with different accents.

WILBER: (Laughing) We fool around a lot.

*   *   *

WILBER: I don't know why you don't believe me when I tell you I'm her half-brother. We grew up in the same family.

JEANNE: But you don't look anything alike! You even talk with different accents.

WILBER: (Laughing) We fool around a lot.

Use the format you prefer; all are accepted ones.

Stage directions are another convention, or accepted method, of writing down information in scripts. Stage directions are instructions to the actor or director regarding what a character does and how he or she does it. The opening of each scene will have a description telling the location, the time of day, and sometimes the date, so you'll know if the play takes place in modern times or many years ago. Some writers give lots of additional information such as the furniture in the room, the lighting, conditions outside affecting the situation. Stage directions also tell what characters are present at the opening of the scene, when someone enters during the scene, and when someone exits. Important pieces of action are very briefly described, as is the way a character behaves or feels. Stage directions are set off from the dialogue by parentheses; sometimes they are written in italics to separate them further from words to be spoken by the characters. Stage directions have been added to the following dialogue.

Scene Three

(The Milgrims' kitchen. It's mid-afternoon the next day. The room is empty and no lights are on; a fierce snowstorm can be seen through the window over the sink.)

JANET
(Entering through the hall door with a wet bag of groceries. She is covered with snow. Calling.) Is

90

anybody here? Hey, Mom! *(She sets bag down on table and pulls off mittens, boots, and hat. DAVID opens the living room door stage left and looks in.)* Where is everybody?

DAVID
Who did you have in mind?

JANET
(Startled) You scared me. Why are the lights out? *(Goes to turn on switch. Nothing happens.)*

DAVID
That's why. The phone is out, too.

The amount of stage directions you give is a matter of personal preference. You want to make things clear to the actors but don't want to burden them with details. Give them only what you think necessary. If you intend a character to be upset and crying when he says a particular line, it helps to say so in a stage direction, as the actor might interpret that line to be said with laughter. However, be economical with directions regarding the character's emotional reactions; performing artists appreciate as much freedom of interpretation as possible. Background information given on the character or the setting will vary from playwright to playwright. Shakespeare gave almost no stage directions: Enter, Exit, A Castle, a Battleground were the extent of it. George Bernard Shaw, another famous British playwright, on the other hand, gave pages of stage directions describing the characters and the situation.

Actors' scripts need wide margins and a blank facing page

91

so actors can pencil in directions that they and the director have devised—when to sit on a couch, for instance—rather than to leave such moves to actors' improvisation. The movement that the actors make onstage is called blocking. It is rare for the playwright to ask for particular blocking because she or he would have no way of knowing if productions of the play were to be performed on a large stage or a small one, on a stage with the audience sitting out in front (proscenium setting) or with the audience circling the stage (in the round). It is the job of the director and actors to work this out and pencil in (in case they later want to make changes) these instructions on the margin of the page or on the blank facing page.

Areas of the stage are a convention in theater that the playwright may use if he or she wants. They have been worked out to make things clearer for the actors, the director, the designers, and anyone else working on the production. The part of the stage that is used for acting and can be seen by the audience is called, quite naturally, onstage. The areas close by but out of sight of the audience are called backstage or offstage. The backstage area is the place actors wait prior to making their entrances and the **set, props,** and costume changes are kept in readiness for use in the coming scenes. The offstage areas to the right and left of a stage that an audience faces are called the wings. If the audience sits in the round, the wings are behind the audience and reached by aisles through the seating area.

In a proscenium setting, downstage is the area closest to the audience; upstage would be the part farthest back from them. Center stage is just where you'd imagine. Upstage center is in the middle against the back wall, and downstage center on the front center edge. Stage right and stage left are from the actor's point of view. So, if you're in the audience looking at the stage, the area onstage to your right would be called stage left, as all directions are for the actors rather than the audience. The playwright would use these directions if he or she felt it were important to state where onstage things happen. You can also use it as a kind of shorthand, as it is easier to state (LION enters SL; RABBIT sees him and runs off SR) rather than (LION enters one side of the stage; RABBIT sees him and runs off the other). Having made a choice, however, realize that directors and actors will often ignore what you indicate in this regard.

Directions for performing in the round, or for arena staging, are given in terms either of a compass (North, South, East, West) or a clock (12:00, 3:00, etc.). Because more people are familiar with the face of a clock than with the face of a compass, I find the use of hours more practical.

A time saving suggestion for getting your written script into its final form is to cut and paste. It can be frustrating to copy your work over and over for each change you make in it. Try making a photocopy of it and using this copy to mark up, cut up, and rearrange onto a blank page. Keep the original intact to refer to in case you lose track of the various pieces. It is easier to make your final, clean copy from a paste-up that is in the proper order than to try to follow arrows and notes for inserts on messy originals. Minimize drudge work whenever possible!

••• 14 •••

You as Playwright

By now I'm sure you no longer think of playwriting as just making up things for actors to say. You can see how you must visualize the whole event and how it's going to work onstage. I have suggested that this is easier to do when you have people act out the scenes as you're working on the script. Seeing the characters in action can help you shape ideas for your play. But having others help you with your play can bring up the question: Whose play is it? When you're writing off by yourself, there's no question that the script is yours. You thought it through and wrote it down. But if you have collaborated with other writers, with a director, or with actors, it might be confusing to determine whose piece it is.

Someone must have the final word in writing the play. If it was your idea to start with, it should remain yours. Make this clear at the start when you ask for anyone's input. No matter how many people contribute to a piece, the final choices need to be made by you, the playwright, in order to keep your vision for the piece intact. If you find that you are getting too many suggestions or that others seem to be taking your idea off on a different track, remind them that this one is your play and they may write their own in another way. You have probably heard the old saying, "Too many cooks spoil the broth." The cooking comparison works here again; too many playwrights will spoil any play.

As a playwright you are a creator or a "worker." This is why the name for the person doing it is not spelled play-write but PLAYWRIGHT. Wright is an old-fashioned word meaning a person who works. It was used with other tasks as well, like cartwright (one who makes carts) or shipwright (one who makes or repairs ships). The term implies that a complicated task is involved and it requires skill and making adjustments until the product is finished properly. When you build things, there is three-dimensional shaping, not just a straight list of things to do. There is a process. There is also a sense of something happening, bubbling up, fermenting, as with yeast that makes bread dough rise, or with natural grape juice that ferments and "works" and is transformed into wine.

So it is with you as you work your play. Work it until it is the way you want it and you feel it "works" for you and an audience. When a play works, it becomes the fermenting agent, the thing that makes the viewer's imagination and feelings bubble up. Working plays and getting them to work is no easy task, but it's a satisfying one and lots of fun. I love it because it's a more exciting way to express ideas than just talking and because it's exhilarating to create a project that brings together many people to work cooperatively. It's also a chance to make a picture of the world the way I want it for a change!

GLOSSARY

action. What a character does to get what her or she wants. It is what happens in a play, caused by characters interacting and changing. It is the means by which a play tells its story.

actor. The person who becomes a character in a play and makes this character become alive on stage. Someone who acts.

antagonist. The character in a play who stands in the way of the main character's getting what he or she wants, thereby creating the main conflict in the play.

beginning action. The first major event in a play brought about by the main character doing something that changes the opening situation and starts the main action of the play.

blocking. The pattern of movement onstage made by actors playing the scenes of a play. These decisions about where to sit, stand, walk, and do various activities are made by the director and/or the actors, usually not the playwright.

business. See **stage business.**

character. A person in a story or a play. In plays, characters are brought to life by the actors. Although characters are not always human (such as animals or objects or gods or ogres), they usually symbolically stand for people or an exaggerated human quality.

climax. The highest point of the play in which we see the principal characters dealing with the consequences of their actions. The action of the play comes to a head in the climax, answering the main question of the play.

cold reading. See **a reading.**

collaborating. Working cooperatively with someone on a creative project.

crisis. The point of highest tension in the play just before the climax in which the most important issue hangs in a balance. The crisis is broken by the main character deciding to do something that moves the action directly into the climax to end the play.

critique. To look critically at a creative work, weighing its strong points and its weak points. To evaluate.

development. The unfolding of the plot line through actions by the characters that cause new things to happen, which in turn lead the characters to new actions.

dialogue. The words in a play or a story spoken by the characters.

director. The person who works with the actors to bring a play alive onstage. Once a play moves into production, the director is the main person in charge, and it is his or her interpretation of the script that is final, as long as it doesn't go against the playwright's meaning. If the production of a play is intended to help the playwright fine-tune his or her play, the director needs to work carefully with the playwright to help this process occur.

draft. A completed version of a play that still needs testing, rewriting, and polishing. A rough draft needs lots of work. A first draft is the first version; it may be close to or far from the finished form.

exposition. The opening of the play in which we learn the important background information for the events that will follow.

form. The shape, the organization, the structure of something. It may be an external shape, such as the curved outside of a vase, or it could be the way something is organized, such as the rules of a game. In works of art like a play it means the manner in which the parts are put together to make a whole creation. In a play or story, those parts are the elements of characters, action, activities, and settings.

improvisation. Acting in rehearsal or performance without planned dialogue. Sometimes the action and the plot are not planned either. All theater improvisations need some guiding rules that are planned in advance, however, to enable the players to make the scene hold together.

improvise. To act without a script or knowing in advance how everything will happen. To make decisions moment to moment, using what is available.

lines. The words spoken by characters in a play. The term is usually used instead of dialogue when thought of from the actor's point of view as an element to work with in rehearsal and performance.

locale. See **location.**

location. The place in which a scene occurs. It could be the living room of a house or a beach or the cabin of an airplane. Also called **locale.**

motivation. The reason behind a character's wanting to do something. It could be a feeling or an idea, complicated or simple.

objective. What a person wants to do. In a play it is what the character wants. Sometimes objectives are called intentions. For the playwright it would be what she or he wants to say with the play.

the opening. The beginning of a play in which we are introduced to enough background information to help us understand the events that follow. Also called **exposition.**

piece. A part of something larger. "A costume piece" means part of the whole costume, such as a policeman's hat would be a piece of the policeman's costume; it can also mean a single costume element that represents the whole costume, such as a policeman's hat being used to signify a whole policeman's costume when the actors are dressed in neutral clothing like jeans and sweat shirts.

Artists use the term "piece" to indicate the work they are currently creating, such as a dance, a mime, a musical composition, or a play. Using "piece" instead of "play" for your script usually implies it is a work that is still being formed or has just recently been created.

playwright. A person who creates a play. The word "wright" means worker. It used to be used in connection with a variety of crafts, for example: wheelwright (a person who makes wheels), shipwright (you guessed it!), wainwright (can you look it up?). The wright is a person who works the play, not just writes it.

playwriting. The creative act of writing a play. It doesn't literally have to involve writing it down, but it usually does. It involves creating characters; giving structure to the action; defining locations; giving characters actions, motivations, and lines; and making the meaning of the play clear.

plot. The key events that happen to characters in a story or a play.

premise. The basic idea underlying your play, which is presented through the action of the characters in the development of the plot.

producer. The person in charge of getting a play ready to perform, coordinating the efforts of director, actors, designers, publicity people. In professional theater, this person is also responsible for raising the money and paying all expenses.

production. The event of a performance or preparing for a performance of a play when theatrical elements of stage sets, costumes, lighting, sound, and so forth are used.

props. Abbreviation for properties. These are any small objects used by actors in their performance. They could be part of the set, such as a water pitcher on the table, or a hand prop, such as a deck of cards a character keeps in his pocket for an onstage game.

protagonist. The main character in a play, whose story it is. The one who gets things moving.

a reading. The presentation of a play in which actors read from scripts but do not memorize lines or go through the actions. Sets are not used. Sometimes readings are given as actual performances with actors in costume, lit by theatrical lights. Usually readings are used to give the playwright or director or producer a sense of how the script is working. A **cold reading** is one done by actors who are seeing the script for the first time.

rehearsal. Practice work to prepare the play for performance. It is the time when actors (and director, if there is one) work together to create the characters physically, plan the action, set the blocking, learn the lines (unless the play is to be improvised), and coordinate all the elements to be used, such as music, dance, costumes, set, props.

resolution. The ending of the play after the climax. Here we see how the characters are going to handle the events that have just happened to them. In the closing the playwright makes his or her final point about the main question or issue of the play. Sometimes called denouement.

scenario. A brief description of the events that occur in a specific scene and the characters involved. Used by playwrights to outline how they will break down events of the plot into specific scenes. Used by actors improvising a scene to remind them what action to include.

scene. A division of the play that occurs in one physical location during which something happens to the characters to move the plot along. A very short play will have only one scene. Long plays have several. Plays that last over an hour usually group the scenes into acts.

scenery. The physical pieces used to create a specific location for a scene. It can be very realistic in creating the illusion of a forest or an office. It can be neutral such as plain drapes or screens. It includes objects actors use such as couches, tables, stairs, trees, and so forth.

script. The written version of a play. It tells the reader what characters are involved, in what settings the action occurs, what words the characters say, often their state of mind, and a brief statement of the action.

secondary character. The character in a play with whom the main character is principally involved, about whom the main character cares most. The main character's relationship with the secondary character is usually complicated by the antagonist.

a set. The scenery created for the play.

to set. To establish a fixed way of doing something.

setting. The physical location in which a scene occurs.

sketch. A short, theatrical presentation that is not a complete scene or play. It could be just one character talking to the audience or doing something. It could be a little mood piece or a funny piece of action between two or a few characters.

stage business. Activity onstage done by the actors as part of their characters' activity or action. For instance, setting the table, falling down, or getting dressed.

stage directions. Instructions to the reader, director, actor by the playwright about what the characters are doing and about where things are happening.

supporting characters. Characters who fill out the play, adding to situations in which the primary and secondary characters and the antagonist are playing the main action.

work. To apply effort to a task in order to accomplish something desired. To accomplish the desired effect, as when a play works.

SELECTED BIBLIOGRAPHY

Sources of Plays by Young People

Children's Radio Theatre, 1314 14th Street, NW, Washington, D.C. 20005. Radio plays by children and youth available in either script form or audio tape cassettes. Write for catalogue to order specific titles. Annual Henny Penny Playwriting Contest to which scripts may be submitted by 5- to 17-year-olds.

Dobama Theatre, 1846 Coventry Road, Cleveland Heights, Ohio 44118. Booklet of prize-winning plays by seven to seventeen-year-olds published annually. Picture and short biography of each playwright included. Available by writing to address above.

Meeting the Winter Bikerider and Other Winning Plays, edited by Wendy Lamb. New York: Dell Publishing Co., 1986. Collection of prize-winning plays from the 1983–84 National Young Playwrights Festival. Scripts by ten- to eighteen-year-olds. Available in bookstores or libraries.

The National Young Playwrights Festival, Foundation of the Dramatists Guild, 234 West 44th Street, New York, New York 10036. Center that promotes playwriting by young people. Runs annual contest to which scripts may be submitted. Also a source for playwriting workshops for young people and of plays by them. Inquiries about festival rules, winning plays, and workshops can be made to the address above.

Young Playwright's Festival Collection, edited by the Foundation of the Dramatists Guild, Inc. New York: Avon Bard, 1982. Paperback collection containing prize-winning plays by high-school-age writers, plus one by a third grader. First publication of plays from the annual contest.

Young Playwrights, 2301 East Franklin Avenue, Minneapolis, Minnesota 55406. Center that fosters playwriting by young people. Runs annual conference for twelve- to nineteen-year-old playwrights to learn from one another and from professionals in workshop setting. Starting a playwriting contest. Inquire about scripts, workshops, and contest by writing to address above.

Books on Improvisation for Young People and Adults

Byers, Ruth. *Creating Theater from Idea Through Performance with Children and Teens.* San Antonio: Trinity University Press, 1968. Good examples of working from original ideas, from stories, or from adult plays through to original scripts. Complete scripts of nine original plays created this way by children and teens included in second half of book. Clear statement of philosophy and goals; helpful suggestions for structuring and focusing sessions. Discussion of variations in approach for different age groups.

Brandes, Donna and Philips, Howard. *Gamesters' Handbook.* London: Hutchinson Co., Ltd., 1977. An easy-to-read collection of theater games for simple theater activities. Divided into sections of improvisations to develop concentration, imagination, personal and social awareness. Descriptions of set-ups for improvisations understandable for young people or adults with little theater background.

Hodgson, John and Richards, Ernest. *Improvisation.* London: Methuen, 1966. Written for adults but usable by young people willing to skip through, picking and choosing helpful suggestions. Useful chapter on "Building a Play from Improvisation" with discussion of a variety of approaches. Some of the references assume familiarity with classical plays *(Oedipus, Romeo and Juliet, A Man for All Seasons, Luther)*, but suggestions are helpful even with skipping these parts, if reader does not have this background. Opening chapters on philosophy behind using improvisation. Major sections on using improv without a text and on using improv to explore a script. Examples of sessions for various age group; chapters on activities to develop various acting skills, such as concentration, spontaneity, imagination, dramatic shaping, communication, and characterization.

Johnstone, Keith. *Impro: Improvisation and the Theatre.* London: Methuen, 1981. A stimulating book for the leader who has had some experience with groups and with drama or has the willingness to jump right into the process. Honest sharing of a British theater artist's work with creating theater, including his philosophy and techniques for working with actors. Specific exercises described. Sections focus on status between characters, spontaneity in playing, narrative skills, and use of masks and trance.

Klein, Maxine. *Theatre for the 98%.* Boston: South End Press, 1978. Written for adults but useful to young people willing to guess at or skip unfamiliar vocabulary. Designed to expand our definitions of theater or plays. Many suggestions for theatrical events based on our own experiences, feelings, and ideas; on current events and political observations; and on our urge to have fun and celebrate. A nontraditional approach to making plays, drama, and theatrical events.

McCaslin, Nellie. *Creative Drama in the Classroom,* fourth edition. New York: Longman, 1984. Well-known text on philosophy behind and an overview of the variety of ways creative drama is used in school settings. Although written for adults with much of the material geared to early elementary grades, there are many suggestions and complete stories

104

that adolescents and teens could have fun with, especially if they want to practice with some easier material or prepare plays to perform for younger audiences. Excellent bibliography of books in the field.

Scher, Anna and Verrall, Charles. *100 + Ideas for Drama.* London: Heinemann Educational Books, 1975. Short, easy book for young people or adults wanting to do informal drama. Brief introductory chapter for adults on the philosophy and techniques of setting up drama classes, followed by description of many activities for improvisation: physical games, mental games, speaking games, story building, mime, movement, warm-up activities, character work, prop and costume activities, as well as many suggestions for plots for situation dramas and improvised plays.

Spolin, Viola. *Improvisation for the Theatre.* Evanston: Northwestern University Press, 1963. The classic book of improvisation using game structure. Hundreds of theater games described by the master improv teacher. The philosophy behind this approach to improvisation should help its users develop their own games or variations on ones described. The format is sometimes confusing to understand until one is in the process of using the material. Playing the games is the best method of understanding this approach.

Spolin, Viola. *Theatre Games for Rehearsals, A Director's Handbook.* Evanston: Northwestern University Press, 1985. Specific application of theater games to the rehearsal process. Helpful in understanding Spolin's philosophy of improvisation and for keeping any performance alive and in the present. Could help writers and directors not only get lively, engaged performances of their script but also give playwrights insights for improving a script that's being written.

Stewig, John Warren. *Informal Drama in the Elementary Language Arts Program.* New York: Teachers College Press, Columbia University, 1983. A book for teachers by an experienced classroom teacher who clearly understands and supports the creative process. Responsive to need for both open exploration and well-articulated goals. Discusses approaches for different age groups, specific lesson plans, suggestions for avoidance of trouble, and political strategies to use with peers, supervisors, and parents to elicit support for the work. Excellent annotated references for books, articles, films, visual aids.

Wilder, Rosilyn. *A Space Where Anything Can Happen.* Rowayton, Connecticut: New Plays Books, 1977. A good aid to teachers and leaders working with city middle-school students. The approach is still valid despite the fast-changing population. Student readers might find the chapter "Let Us Be Free" inspiring in its description of how a simple improvisation led to an extended film project about slavery and today's dreams of a just society.

Selected Scripts for Young Audiences by Contemporary Playwrights Based on Well-Known Stories from Literature or Folktales

Atkins, Flora. *Skupper-Duppers.* New Plays, Inc., 1975. Dramatization of sea tales from Alaskan Eskimos, Hawaiian Mauis, Virgin Island West Indians, and Puerto Ricans. For eight or nine actors with singing participation from audience.

Bronson, Bernice. *In the Beginning.* New Plays, Inc., 1971. A blended dramatization of several creation myths from around the world for six players and planned audience participation.

Carle, Susan. *Rikki-Tikki-Tavi.* Dramatic Publishing Co., 1978. A dramatic adaptation of Rudyard Kipling's telling of the tale in his *Just So Stories* of East Indian folktales. Ten human and animal characters. Traditional presentational style.

Goldberg, Moses. *Hansel and Gretel.* New Plays, Inc., 1972. Theatrical, commedia dell'arte treatment of the well-known Grimm fairy tale, for a company of six performers with some audience participation.

Jennings, Coleman. *The Honorable Urashima Taro.* Dramatic

Publishing Co., 1972. Dramatization of a Japanese fantasy tale of a fisherman's reward of a princely life under the sea that is shattered on his return to his changed village. Eleven or more players.

Korty, Carol. *Plays from African Folktales.* Scribner's, 1975 (available through Baker's Plays). Four dramatizations of tales from the Nuer, Hausa, Ashanti, and Yoruba people of Africa. For eight to twenty players with dance and music called for.

Koste, Virginia Glasgow. *The Trial of Tom Sawyer.* Anchorage, 1983. A play based on incidents from Mark Twain's story that lead to Tom's trial and growing up. Mark Twain serves as narrator. For up to twenty-seven actors.

Kraus, Joanna. *The Dragon Hammer and The Tale of Oniroku.* New Plays, Inc., 1977. Two short plays for the very young; the first from a Korean folktale, the second from a Japanese tale. For a few, a dozen, or more actors depending on staging.

Lacey, Jackson. *The Prince, The Wolf, and The Firebird.* Anchorage Press, 1972. A large cast play for twenty or more players by a British playwright dramatizing this ancient Russian fairy tale. A fanciful, pagent style play of fourteen scenes.

Levy, Jonathan. *The Marvelous Adventures of Tyl.* New Plays, 1973. A commedia dell'arte style script for an ensemble of seven players about the legendary medieval German prankster, Tyll Eulenspiegel.

Nanus, Susan. *The Phantom Tollbooth.* Samuel French, Inc., 1977. A two-act play based on the popular book by Norton Juster for a large cast of nineteen to thirty-seven actors in five fantasy settings.

Schneider, Hansjorg. *Robinson and Friday.* Translated by Ken and Barbi Rugg, edited and adapted by Carol Korty. Baker's Plays, 1980. A fanciful play for four characters very loosely based on Defoe's novel *Robinson Crusoe* with its own message.

Scott, Dennis. *Sir Gawain and the Green Knight*. Anchorage Press in association with The National Theatre of the Deaf, 1978. A play drawn from the ancient legend of King Arthur focusing on the testing of Gawain. Written by a Jamaican playwright for a company of six to twenty actors.

Sills, Paul. *Story Theatre*. Samuel French, Inc., 1971. The original script that set the definition of story theatre for work to follow. Simple, witty interpretation of a string of Grimm's fairy tales and Aesop's fables created for an ensemble of seven actors.

Stokes, Jack. *Wiley and the Hairy Man*. Adapted for stage by Alice Stokes. Coach House Press, 1970, 1977. A choral reading script based on American tale from the South that has been adapted for physical staging for six or more actors. Emphasis on poetry and sound of words.

Zeder, Suzan. *Wiley and the Hairy Man*. Anchorage Press, 1978. Dramatization of the same tale by another playwright demonstrating different treatment of the dramatic structure. Four main characters and chorus of four or more.

Major Publishers of Plays for Young People

Anchorage Press, P.O. Box 8067, New Orleans, Louisiana 70182

Baker's Plays, 100 Chauncy Street, Boston, Massachusetts 02111

Coach House Press, Inc., 53 West Jackson Blvd., Chicago, Ill. 60604

Dramatic Publishing Co., 4150 No. Milwaukee Ave., Chicago, Ill. 60641

New Plays, Incorporated, Box 273, Rowayton, Connecticut 06853

Samuel French, 25 West 45th Street, New York, New York 10036

Books on Approaches to Teaching Writing

Calkins, Lucy McCormick. *The Art of Teaching Writing*. Portsmouth, N.H.: Heinemann Educational Books, Inc., 1986. An inspiring and practical book for adults by an experienced

108

writer and teacher, a member of Columbia Teachers College Writing Project. Offers good perspective on shift in teaching of writing over past fifteen years to emphasis on process over product. Author works below surface issues of stimulating ideas to getting students "deeply and personally involved in writing." Her approach nurtures the artist in herself and in others. Book does not specifically deal with playwriting, but the philosophy and specific suggestions are appropriate and helpful to playwriting.

Graves, Donald H., *Writing: Teachers and Children at Work*. Portsmouth, N.H.: Heinemann Educational Books, 1983. A helpful guide for teachers by a master teacher on the process approach to writing. Direct style of writing with ample examples of model dialogues between teacher and students. Focus on setting up constructive plans for working, effective questioning, providing support for student growth, and appropriate teaching of standards. Principles applicable to writing plays and to teaching teens and adults.

Hansen, Jane; Thomas, Newkirk; and Graves, Donald. *Breaking Ground: Teachers Relate Reading and Writing in the Elementary School.* Porstmouth, N.H.: Heinemann Educational Books, Inc., 1985. Book for adults devoted to sharing a new philosophy and technique of teaching literacy. The few chapters focusing on junior-high-level work, as well as the many on early elementary level, convey an approach that nurtures the creative process. No specific reference to form of playwriting, but much discussion of the child artist's conceptual development and value of feedback on work from writer, teacher, and peers. Excellent bibliography of other books in the field.

Lopate, Phillip. *Being with Children*. Garden City, N.Y.: Doubleday and Co., Inc., 1975. Fascinating, well-written personal account of an artist's endeavor to connect with students and teachers in a traditional school setting in the early 1970s. Focus is primarily on poetry and prose, but some sections on scripts, videotaping, and play production. Author is member of Teachers and Writers Collaborative in New York City; honest with self and sets model for being honest with kids. Good variety of suggestions for stimuli for creative work, many of which can be adapted to writing in play form.

Sohn, David. *Pictures for Writing: The Stop, Look, and Write Series, A Visual Approach to Composition.* New York: Bantam Books, 1969. An interesting little paperback for young people or adults of black and white photographs arranged with notes to spark the writer's imagination. Easy to adapt the suggestions to playwriting form. Good starting place for using other photos, paintings, art objects, junk objects, snatches of conversation, and so forth to stimulate ideas.

Books for Adults on Playwriting

Egri, Lajos. *The Art of Dramatic Writing.* New York: Simon and Schuster, 1960. Enjoyable book in which author talks informally with reader about elements of playwriting, often using question and answer technique. Clear discussion of premise, character, plot structure. Uses slightly different terminology at times and unorthodox analysis of protagonist in some examples. Liberal use of sections of dialogue from well-known plays to illustrate his points.

Grebanier, Bernard. *Playwriting: How To Write for the Theatre.* New York: Harper and Row, Publishers, Inc., 1961. Clearly written, readable book on the focus and structure of plays. Thorough discussion of elements of plot, characterization, dialogue with many helpful examples from a variety of outstanding, well-known plays. Comparisons between story and drama, comedy and tragedy in drama, appropriate focuses for full-length plays and one-act plays. Suggestions for writing exercises related to the various elements discussed.

Smiley, Sam. *Playwriting: The Structure of Action.* Englewood Cliffs, N.J.: Prentice-Hall, Inc., 1971. Detailed, analytical book starting with chapters on a writer's vision and the process of writing a play and moving into many fine points of the structure of plays. Discussion of plot, character, use of words and languages; comparisons of various forms of drama, such as melodrama and didactic drama, which may be more relevant classifications for contemporary plays than classical comedy and tragedy. Discussion of production styles in writing, as well as production issues for performance and marketing issues for selling scripts.

INDEX

Index